Donald Barthelme

**A COMPREHENSIVE BIBLIOGRAPHY
AND ANNOTATED SECONDARY CHECKLIST**

DONALD BARTHELME. *Photograph by Jerry Bauer. Courtesy Farrar, Straus and Giroux.*

DONALD BARTHELME

A Comprehensive Bibliography
and Annotated Secondary Checklist

Jerome Klinkowitz
Asa Pieratt
Robert Murray Davis

ARCHON BOOKS
1977

Library of Congress Cataloging in Publication Data

Klinkowitz, Jerome.
   Donald Barthelme.

   Includes index.
   1. Barthelme, Donald—Bibliography. I. Pieratt, Asa B.,
joint author. II. Davis, Robert Murray, joint author.
Z8076.76.K55   [PS3552.A76]   016.818′5′ 409   77-12966
ISBN 0-208-01712-7

©The Shoe String Press, Inc. 1977
First published 1977 as an Archon Book, an imprint of
THE SHOE STRING PRESS, INC.
Hamden, Connecticut 06514

All rights reserved
Printed in the United States of America

CONTENTS

Preface	7
A Donald Barthelme Chronology	13
Abbreviations	17
Definitions	19
A. Books by Donald Barthelme	23
B. Short Stories and Fictional Parodies	49
C. Essays	61
D. Dramatic Adaption of a Work	63
E. Interviews with Donald Barthelme	65
F. Sound Recordings of Donald Barthelme	67
G. Early Writings in Houston, Texas	69
H. Bibliographies of Donald Barthelme	105
I. Annotated Checklist of Critical Essays on Donald Barthelme	107

J. Reviews of Books by Donald Barthelme 117

K. Publicly Disavowed Forgeries of Stories
    Allegedly Written by "Donald Barthelme" 123

Index 125

PREFACE

Donald Barthelme (b. 1931) has been called one of the most significant writers in America by both literary quarterlies and national news magazines, a distinction which few avant-gardists share. Through his regular exposure in *The New Yorker* and his occasional appearances in smaller magazines, Barthelme has educated a readership to the intricacies of innovative American fiction, of which he is one of the leading practitioners. This bibliography offers full descriptions of his books, stories (some of which were pseudonymous or unsigned at publication), essays, dramatic adaptations, sound recordings, interviews, juvenalia, and the critical commentaries on them, plus all available information on the foreign editions of his work, in a manner to suit the needs of collectors, literary scholars, and students of his writing.

Barthelme's national career began in late 1962, when he took up residence in New York City to edit the art and literature journal, *Location,* for Thomas Hess and Harold Rosenberg. On March second of the next year, his story "L'Lapse" appeared in *The New Yorker,* beginning an association with that magazine which has been the foundation of Barthelme's fame. But before moving North, Barthelme had served a long journalistic and editorial apprenticeship in his home town of Houston, Texas, writing for his college newspaper and magazine, working as a reporter for the Houston *Post,* serving as director for the Contemporary Arts Museum, and founding the University of Houston *Forum,* an ambitious journal which featured contributions by Barthelme and by such prominent authors as Alain Robbe-Grillet, Leslie Fiedler, Hugh Kenner, and William H. Gass. This bibliography contains a special section, researched by Robert Murray Davis, which details Barthelme's work from this Houston period, excluding only his high school journalism which cannot be listed with any authority or completeness; the period covered is, however, complete.

Among the major categories of this bibliography are full descriptions of Donald Barthelme's booklength publications in the United States, including complete bibliographical information, printing histories, variations in advance galleys, and contents. In addition, all available information on the foreign editions of Barthelme's work is included; the compilers have examined copies of nearly all these foreign editions, and have indicated the few instances where descriptions are second hand. Printing histories of foreign editions are included in all cases where the authors could locate the information. Unfortunately, some foreign publishers failed to respond to our queries and still others have a policy which forbids release of these figures even when the author requests that they be released. Separate categories list Barthelme's essays, dramatic adaptations, sound recordings, plus bibliographies, critical checklistings, and major reviews (when they could be located) of his books. Interviews with Barthelme and critical commentaries on his works are listed by author, and are abstracted and cross-indexed according to subjects discussed. A special section lists forged stories falsely attributed to "Donald Barthelme," but the authenticity of which have been disavowed.

The limits of this bibliography's coverage extend from Barthelme's juvenalia beginning in 1948, and include his mature work to December 31, 1976, following the publication of his story collection, *Amateurs*.

Booklength Works

For each title we have cited all editions, printings, review editions (or copies), and any special editions. The arrangement under each title is chronological within each of the following groups: first, all American Editions; second, all British Editions; and third, all other foreign editions. Within each of these groups, the items cited are arranged by date of publication with review copies or special editions being cited in the notes to the edition of which it is a part. For each entry, if possible, the authors provide: (1) a description of the title page; (2) a collation paragraph; (3) a binding and description paragraph; and (4) a printing history. In those instances where the authors were unable to gather complete information for an item, the information which was located is provided in the preceding format where applicable. For a number of foreign language editions the only information noted was a citation in a national bibliography or *Index Translationum*. For these items we have simply cited the information located without comment.

In order to distinguish each edition, the authors have used terms as defined in the American National Standards for Title Leaves of a Book. [See "Definitions."] These definitions were used because traditional terminology leads to confusion, now that so many books are produced and reproduced by photo offset. For example, under traditional rules the Delta paperback edition of *Guilty Pleasures*, which was published in 1976, is called the first edition, even though this title was first published by Farrar, Straus and Giroux in 1974. It is called the first edition because the text is a photo-reproduced copy of the Farrar printing. Hence, with modern printing techniques, under traditional rules first editions could be made at any time and regardless of the number of intervening editions. Under the terminology we have adopted, this Delta edition becomes the "Delta Re-Edition of the First Edition," thus avoiding the confusion of traditional terminology.

Our book descriptions follow this formula:

1. Title paragraph

    The title paragraph provides, line by line, an exact description of the material appearing on the title page. Each line is separated from the following by a slash (/) mark. For things other than words or standard punctuation which appear on the page, the authors place a description or explanation within square brackets ([   ]). If a slash line (/) itself appears on a title page, the authors indicate it by saying "[slash]" since this notation is used to indicate lines.

2. Collation paragraph

    The collation paragraph describes page by page the contents of the book. In this paragraph the authors cite that information from the verso of the title page which distinguishes it as the first printing of the edition cited. Also from this page, information relating to the printing history of the book and the translator's name are noted if they do not appear elsewhere in the descriptive paragraphs. These citations are made using the same line by line method outlined in number one above for description of the title page.

3. Contents paragraph

For collections the authors include a contents paragraph. This is simply a title listing of the stories included in the collection, in the order in which they appear. Any changes in contents from the first edition of a collection are noted in the notes for that edition.

4. Binding and description paragraph

In this paragraph the authors cite the following: (1) the size of a signature in centimeters giving the length then width; (2) type of binding and color; i.e., cloth over boards or wraps; (3) for items in wraps, the colors used are named except where there are more than five, and then only the number of colors is given; (4) the wording on the spine; unless otherwise stated it is to be assumed that the stamping is parallel to the spine of the book and will be noted as reading from either top to bottom (abbreviated T-B), or from bottom to top (abbreviated B-T); if a word or a group of words reads horizontally, this is noted by placing a slash on either side of the word(s) and an "H" in parenthesis precedes the word(s); (5) the name of the designer of the DJ; (6) the description of the DJ to the extent needed to either identify it, or to distinguish the edition; (7) the presence and color of end papers; (8) the price at which the volume was originally issued; and (9) a statement as to color of and whether or not the edges have been trimmed.

5. Printing history paragraph

This paragraph lists the dates and number of copies of each printing.

6. Notes

In the notes the authors cite: (1) typographical errors; (2) information regarding review editions or copies including descriptions of these items if available; and (3) other information deemed necessary.

Donald Barthelme cooperated with all aspects of this bibliography and deserves our gratitude. Special thanks are also due to Robert Giroux, Roger W. Straus, Jr., Jane Anderson and *The New Yorker*, Bonnie Bryant (for obtaining foreign editions), and Julie Huffman (for arranging the manuscript).

JEROME KLINKOWITZ
ASA PIERATT
ROBERT MURRAY DAVIS

A DONALD BARTHELME CHRONOLOGY

1931	Born April 7, Philadelphia.
1933	Moves with family to Houston, Texas.
1945-6	"Literary" reporter for *The Eagle,* St. Thomas High School, Houston, Texas.
1946	Honorable mention for short story in *Scholastic Magazine* contest, Junior division.
1946-7	"Features" reporter, *The Eagle.*
1947-8	"Features" reporter, *The Eagle.*
1948-9	Wins Poet Laureate of Texas Award for "Inertia." Ties for fourth place in *Scholastic Magazine* short story competition with "Integrity Cycle." Associate editor, *Sequoyha 1948-49,* the literary magazine of Lamar High School. September. Enrolls at the University of Houston; skips the spring of 1950; enrolled continuously through fall, 1952; then, with interruptions, from spring 1955 through second summer session, 1957. Final Standing: junior.
1950	June 16. First contribution to the *Cougar,* University of Houston student newspaper, for which he writes both under his own name, and the pen-name "Bardley." July 21. Assignment editor, *Cougar.* August 11. Assignment editor and copy reader, *Cougar.* September 22. Amusements editor, *Cougar;* responsible for content and makeup of the back page.

	September. On script committee, Varsity Varieties, a show sponsored by student publications.
1951	February 13. Managing editor, *Cougar*.
	March 1—July 13. Works for University of Houston News Service.
	April 20—May 25. Editor in Chief, *Cougar*, for six issues.
	July 15. Began working for the Houston *Post*.
1953	February. To the Army: Fort Polk, Japan, Korea. Worked on an Army newspaper.
1955	January 16. First post-Army article in Houston *Post*.
	September 30. Resigns from *Post;* begins working for the University of Houston News Service under Farris Block.
1956	Succeeds Block as editor of *Acta Diurna*, weekly newsletter for the University of Houston faculty and staff.
	August 8. Last listed as editor on masthead of *Acta Diurna*.
	September. First issue of *Forum*, Barthelme editor.
1959	On board of directors and exhibition committee, Contemporary Arts Museum.
1960	Vice President in charge of Public Relations, Contemporary Arts Association.
	First national publication, review in *The Reporter*.
	Spring. Judge of competition for cover design of *Harvest*, University of Houston literary magazine.
	October. Donald W. Lee succeeds Barthelme as editor of *Forum*.
1961	March. Named acting director of Contemporary Arts Museum.
	August 1. Resigns from the University of Houston; becomes director of the Contemporary Arts Museum.
1962	October 1. Resigns as director of Contemporary Arts Museum to edit *Location* in New York.
1963	First publication in *The New Yorker*, "L'Lapse."
1964	First book published, *Come Back. Dr. Caligari*.
1965	First paperback book published, *Come Back, Dr. Caligari*.
1966	First book published in England, *Come Back, Dr. Caligari;* Guggenheim Fellow.

1967	*Snow White.*
1968	*Unspeakable Practices, Unnatural Acts.*
1970	*City Life* published and cited by *The New York Times Book Review* as one of the most important books of 1970.
1971	*The Slightly Irregular Fire Engine* (for children) published, and wins the National Book Award in this category.
1972	*Sadness* published; begins teaching career at State University of New York at Buffalo, replacing John Barth; subsequently teaches at the City University of New York.
1973	Several forged "Barthelme" stories appear in literary journals, are disclaimed by Barthelme.
1974	*Guilty Pleasures.*
1975	*The Dead Father.*
1976	*Amateurs.*

ABBREVIATIONS

A	*Amateurs*
CB	*Come Back, Dr. Caligari*
CL	*City Life*
DF	*The Dead Father*
GP	*Guilty Pleasures*
S	*Sadness*
SW	*Snow White*
UP	*Unspeakable Practices, Unnatural Acts*

DEFINITIONS FROM
AMERICAN NATIONAL STANDARD
FOR TITLE LEAVES OF A BOOK

1 Edition: All those copies of a work produced from one unchanged type image (except for corrections of typographical errors). Includes all impressions, issues, and reprints in which the text is reproduced from the original setting of the type, direct or by other methods, however long a period of years has lapsed since first publication.
2 First Edition: The first publication of an original or translated manuscript.
3 Impression: All those copies of an edition printed at one time. Also called Printing.
4 Issue: Those copies of an edition differing in physical makeup from other copies of the edition or produced by deliberate intent of the publishers for a particular purpose. They are frequently cited on the title page by such terms as "Large Paper Edition," "Limited Edition", "DeLuxe Edition".
5 Leaf: A part of a book consisting of two pages, one on each side. Plural: Leaves.
6 New Edition. *See* Re-Edition.
8 Re-Edition: A publication distinguished from previous editions by changes made in the contents (revised edition) or typographic layout (new edition) or issued by a publisher other than the original publisher. (American National Standard for Compiling Book Publishing Statistics. 239.8-1968.)
9 Revised Edition. *See* Re-Edition.
10 Reprint: A second or later printing of a work which is unchanged in content and layout, apart from corrections of typographical errors in the previous edition, even if several years elapse between printings. A reprint by any publisher other than the original publisher is regarded as a re-edition, although the term "reprint" is frequently used in current publishing practice for such a re-edition.

Donald Barthelme
A COMPREHENSIVE BIBLIOGRAPHY
and Annotated Secondary Checklist

A

BOOKS BY DONALD BARTHELME

AA   COME BACK, DR. CALIGARI

AA1   *First edition 1964.*

Come back, / Dr. Caligari / Donald Barthelme / Little, Brown and Company • Boston • Toronto / .

Collation: pp. 4 leaves + 184, as follows: half title; verso blank; title page as above; selected information from verso as follows: Copyright . . . 1964 BY DONALD BARTHELME / FIRST EDITION / ; dedication; verso blank; Contents; verso blank; text, pp. [1]-[3], 4-183; blank, p. [184].

Contents: Florence Green is 81 / The Piano Player / Hiding Man / Will You Tell Me? / For I'm the Boy Whose Only Joy Is Loving You / The Big Broadcast of 1938 / The Viennese Opera Ball / Me and Miss Mandible / Marie, Marie, Hold On Tight / Up, Aloft in the Air / Margins / The Joker's Greatest Triumph / To London and Rome / A Shower of Gold / .

Binding and description: 19.2 x 13.5 cms. Purple cloth over boards. Spine printed in gold and reads T-B as follows: Donald Barthelme / [parallel and below prior line] Come Back, Dr. Caligari / (H) Little, / (H) Brown / . Milton Glaser designed the dust jacket which is printed in black and purple. Issued at $4.95. White end papers. All edges trimmed. Top edge stained grey.

Note: Two types of galley proofs were distributed in advance of the finished book, one of which consisted of loose pages contained in a box.

AA2   *Anchor edition 1965.*

COME BACK, DR. CALIGARI / [ruled line] / DONALD BARTHELME / Anchor Books / Doubleday & Company, Inc. / Garden City, New York. / .

Collation: pp. 6 leaves + 148, as follows: half title; verso blank; brief biography; verso blank; title page as above; selected information from verso: ANCHOR BOOKS EDITION: 1965 /; dedication; verso blank; Contents; verso blank; text, pp. [1], 2-138; list of other Anchor titles, pp. [139]-[142]; blank, pp. [143]-[148].

Contents: Identical to first edition.

Binding and description: Decorated wraps. Printed in yellow, green, black, blue and white. Designed by Edward Gorey. Spine reads T-B as follows: Come Back, Dr. Caligari Donald Barthelme / (H) Anchor / (H) A / (H) 470 / . Issued at $1.25. All edges trimmed.

/Printing History: First printing, July 1965, 10,000 copies; second printing, 1968, 10,000 copies.

AA3   *Little Brown Quality Paperback edition.*

Come Back, / Dr. Caligari / Donald Barthelme / Little, Brown and Company • Boston • Toronto / .

Collation: pp. 4 leaves + 184, as follows: fly title; verso blank; title page as above; selected information from verso: [copyright line ending as follows] 1964 BY DONALD BARTHELME / [four line rights reserved statement] / C / [ten lines of acknowledgement for permission to reprint] / ; dedication; verso blank; text, pp. [1]-[3], 4-183; blank, p. [184].

Contents: Identical to first edition

Binding and description: 19.7 x 12.7 cms. Decorated wraps. Printed in black, gray and purple. Spine printed in purple and black and reads T-B as follows: [in purple] Donald Barthelme / [in black] Come Back, Dr. Caligari / [in purple] Little Brown / [in black] (H) [publishers monogram] / . Dust jacket designed by Milton Glaser. Issued at $2.25. All edges trimmed.

AA4   *Eyre & Spottiswode edition 1966.*

Come Back, / Dr. Caligari / Donald Barthelme / Eyre & Spottiswode • London / .

Collation: pp. 4 leaves + 184, as follows: Half title; verso blank; title page as above; selected information from verso as follows: [in italics] First published in Great Britain 1966 / by Eyre & Spottiswode (Publishers) Ltd / ; dedication; verso blank; Contents; verso blank; text, pp. [1]-[2], 3-183; blank, p. [184]

Contents: See listing for first edition.

Binding and description: 19.2 x 13.3 cms. Blue paper over boards. Milton Glaser designed the dust jacket.
Spine printed in gold and reads T-B, as follows: Donald / [parallel and below first name] Barthelme / Come Back, Dr. Caligari E & S / . Free end papers. Issued at 18s. All edges trimmed.

Printing History: One printing, 1966, 3,030 copies.

AA5   *Suhrkamp edition 1965.*

Komm Weider, Dr. Caligari. Translated by Hans Wollschläger. Frankfurt: Suhrkamp, 1965. Pp. 196. Issued at 16.80 DM.

Printing History: One printing, 1965, 2,300 copies.

AA6   *Bompiani edition 1967.*

[geometric figure used as design on cover repeated on title page] / DONALD BARTHELME / [in italics] Ritorna, dr. Caligari / [also in italics] Introduzione di Claudio Gorlier / BOMPIANI / .

Collation: pp. 236, as follows: geometric design from cover, p. [1]; blank, p. [2]; I NEOFIGURATIVI / Nuove forme letterarie / BOMPIANI/ , p. [3]; blank, p. [4]; title page as above, p. [5]; selected information from verso as follows: ©1967 Casa Ed. Valentino

Bompiano - Milano / , p. [6]; dedication, p. [7]; blank, p. [8]; text, pp. 9-232; Contents, p. [233]; blank, p. [234]; publishing information, p. [235]; blank, p. [236].

Contents: Introduzione / Florence Green ha ottantun anni / La Pianista / Un uomo si nasconde / Me lo dici? / Sono io il ragazzo la cui unica gioia è amarti / La grande trasmissione del 1938 / Il Ballo dell' Opera di Vienna / Io e Miss Mandible / Marie, Marie, tienti stretta / Sospesi nell'aria / Margini / Il piu grande trionfo del giocatore / A Londra e a Roma / Una pioggia d'oro / .

Binding and description: White paper wraps. Printed in five colors. Spine printed in black and reads T-B as follows: DONALD BAR THELME / [in italics] Ritorna, dr. Caligari / [geometric design] / BOMPIANI / . Issued at 1,600 Lire. All edges trimmed.

AA7   *Suhrkamp edition 1970.*

Donald Barthelme / Komm wieder, Dr. Caligari / Geschichten / Suhrkamp Verlag / .

Collation: pp. 214, as follows: edition suhrkamp / Redaktion: Günther Busch / , p. [1]; brief biography of author, p. [2]; title page as above, p. [3]; selected information from verso as follows: Aus dem Amerikanischen übersetzt von Hans Wollschläger / edition suhrkamp 371 / I.-8. Tausend 1970 / , p. [4]; Contents, p. [5]; blank, p. [6]; dedication, p. [7]; blank, p. [8]; text, pp. 9-172, [173]; blank, p. [174]; description of two other Barthelme titles published by Suhrkamp, p. [175]; lists of other titles published by Suhrkamp, pp. [176]-[183]; suhrkamp wissen, p. [184].

Contents: Florence Green ist 81 / Die Klavier-Spielerin / Ein Mensch versteckt sich / Erzahl doch mal, wie war's denn? / Freunde der Familie / Das grosse Rundfunken von 1938 / Der Wieneropernball / Ich und Miss Mandible / Marie, Marie, halt bloss fest! / Hoch droben in der luft / Randerscheinungen / Des Jokers grösster Triumph / Nach London und Rom / Der Goldregen / .

Binding and description: 17.7 x 10.7 cms. Green wraps. Spine reads T-B as follows: Donald Barthelme Komm wieder, Dr. Caligari 371. Issued at 4.50DM. All edges trimmed.

AA8   *Editorial Anagrama edition 1971.*

Donald Barthelme / Vuelve, Dr. Caligari / [publisher's emblem] / EDITORIAL ANAGRAMA / BARCELONA/ .

Collation: pp. 192, as follows: blank, pp. [1]-[2]; half title, p. [3]; blank, p. [4]; title page as above, p. [5]; selected information from verso as follows: Traduccion: / Jóse Manuel Alvarez y Angela Pérez / ©EDITORIAL ANAGRAMA / , p. [6]; dedication, p. [7]; blank, p. [8]; Introduction by Claudio Gorlier, pp. 9-14; text, pp. [15]-[16], 17-187; blank, p. [188]; Contents, p. [189]; blank, p. [190]; list of other titles in SERIE INFORMAL, p. [191]; blank, p. [192].

Contents: Florence Green tiene 81 anos / El piano / El fugitivo /¿En el barco? / Porque yo soy el muchacho cuya única alegría es amarte / La gran emisora de 1938 / El Baile de la Ópera de Viena / Yo y la señorita Mandible / La manifestación / Alto, muy alto / Margenes / El mayor triunfo del Burlón / Hacia Londres y Roma / Una lluvia de oro / .

Binding and description: 20 x 13 cms. Decorated paper wraps. Printed in purple, maroon and silver over white. Spine printed in purple and reads B-T as follows: [publisher's emblem] / Barthelme / [in italics] Vuelve, dr. Caligari / . Issued at 180 pts. All edges trimmed.

AA9   *Europa Konyvkiado edition 1975.*

DONALD BARTHELME / JÖJJ VISSZA, / DOKTOR / CALIGARI / EUROPA KÖNYVKIADÓ / .

Collation: pp. 172, as follows: series name and number, p. [1]; blank, p. [2]; title page as above, p. [3]; selected information from verso as follows: HUNGARIAN TRANSLATION / © BARTOS TIBOR / , p. [4]; text, pp. 5-167; blank, p. [168]; Contents, p. [169]; blank, p. [170]; publishing information normally found on verso of title page including ISBN 963 07 0279 7, p. [171]; blank, p. [172].

Contents: 81 Lett Florence Green / Zongorista / A Bujdosó / Nekem Mondod? / Jöjj Vissza, Doktor Caligari / A Nagy Adás Harmincnyolcban / En Meg Miss Mandible / Ó, Marie, Ó Marie! / A Bécsi Operabalban / Felhök Felett / Lapszélek / Az Ürge Visszatér / Londonba, Rómába / Aranyesö / Utószó / .

Binding and description: 18.7 x 9.7 cms. Blue paper wraps. Printed in black and white. Spine reads B-T as follows: BARTHELME JOJJ VISSZA, DOKTOR CALIGARI / . Issued at 9.50 Ft. All edges trimmed.

AB SNOW WHITE

AB1   *First edition 1967.*

Donald Barthelme / SNOW WHITE / Atheneum New York / 1967 / .

Collation: pp. 4 leaves + 184, as follows: blank; verso has list of other books by author; half title; verso blank; title page as above; selected information from verso as follows: This book first appeared, in slightly different / form, in the NEW YORKER. Certain portions also / appeared, in different form, in HARPER'S BAZAAR / and PARIS REVIEW. / Copyright©1965, 1967 by Donald Barthelme / First Edition / ; dedication; verso blank; text, pp. [1]-[2], 3-180, [181]; blank, p. [182]; about the author, p. [183]; blank, p. [184].

Binding and description: 20.4 x 12.5 cms. White cloth over boards. Spine reads T-B as follows: Donald Barthelme (in red) / SNOW WHITE (in grey) / Atheneum (in green). Lawrence Ratzkin designed the dust jacket. It is printed in red, blue and black. Issued at $4.50. Red end papers. All edges trimmed. Top edge stained black.

Printing History: First printing, March 1967, 5,000 copies; second printing, July 1967, 3,000 copies.

Note: Two sections of *Snow White* were previously published as stories: "The Affront," *Harper's Bazaar,* 94 (November 1965), 169, 229-230, and "Several Garlic Tales," *Paris Review* #37 (Spring 1966), pp. 62-67. The novel itself was published in the *New Yorker,* 42 (February 18, 1967), occupying continuous pages of most of the issue. Minor changes ensue in the book version, including the apparent restoration of objectionable language.

Note 2: Mr. Barthelme recalls that bound galleys were distributed in advance of the finished book.

AB2   *Bantam edition 1968.*

DONALD BARTHELME / [ruled line] SNOW WHITE / [Bantam emblem] / .

Collation: pp. 4 leaves + 184, as follows: quotes from reviews; list of other titles by author; title page as above; selected information from verso as follows: A BANTAM BOOK [slash] published by arrangement with / Atheneum Publishers / Bantam edition published August

1968 / ; dedication; verso blank; fly title; verso blank; text, pp. [1]-[2], 3-180, [181]; about the author statement, p. [182]; ad for Bantam catalog, p. [183]; blank, p. [184].

Binding and description: 17.8 x 10.5 cms. Decorated wraps. Printed in six colors. Spine printed in black and reads T-B as follows: (H) [Bantam Emblem] / (H) NOVEL(H) [ruled line] / (H) 95¢ / SNOW WHITE / Donald Barthelme / (H) 553 / (H) 07116 / (H) 125 / . Issued at 95¢. All edges trimmed and stained yellow.

Printing History: First printing, August 1968, 154,000 copies; second printing, September 1968, 10,000 copies; third printing, October 1968, 16,000 copies; fourth printing, November 1969, 15,000 copies, fifth printing, July 1971, 16,000 copies; sixth printing, July 1972, 15,000 copies; seventh printing, October 1973, 26,000 copies.

AB3 *Atheneum paper edition 1972.*

[All of title page except the title is printed in italics] Donald Barthelme / SNOW WHITE / Atheneum New York / 1972 / .

Collation: pp. 4 leaves + 184, as follows: blank; verso lists books by author; half title; verso blank; title page as above; selected information from verso as follows: Copyright ©1965, 1967 by Donald Barthelme / Designed by Harry Ford / First Atheneum Paperback Edition / ; dedication; verso blank; text, pp. [1]-[2], 3-180, [181]; blank, p. [182]; three brief paragraphs about the author, p. [183]; blank, p. [184].

Binding and description: 18.4 x 10.8 cms. White paper wraps. Printed in orange and black. Spine reads T-B, as follows: Snow White [slash] Donald Barthelme / Atheneum 191 / . Title and author's name in white. Publishers name and title number in black. Issued at $2.45. All edges trimmed.

Printing History: First and only paper edition, 4,000 copies, August 1972.

AB4 *Cape edition 1968.*

Donald Barthelme / SNOW WHITE / [Cape Emblem] / Jonathan Cape / Thirty Bedford Square London / .

Collation: pp. 4 leaves + 184, as follows: blank; list of other titles by author; half title; blank; title page as above; selected information from verso as follows: First published in Great Britain 1968 / ; dedication; verso blank; text, pp. [1]-[2], 3-180, [181]; blank, p. [182].

Binding and description: 18.6 x 12.5 cms. Black paper over boards. Spine printed in gold and reads T-B as follows: (H) SNOW / (H) WHITE / (H) Donald / (H) Barthelme / (H) [Cape Emblem] / . Dust jacket is white and printed in black and orange. It was designed by Christopher Bradbury. Issued at 21s. White end papers. All edges trimmed. Top edge stained pink.

Printing History: One printing, 1968, 3,000 copies.

AB5   *Panther edition 1971.*

Snow White. London, Panther, 1971. Issued at £0.30. Pp. 181. 18 cms.

Printing History: One printing, July 15, 1971, 25,000 copies.

AB6   *Suhrkamp edition 1968.*

Donald Barthelme / Schneewittchen / Aus dem Amerikanischen von Maria Bosse-Sporleder [in italics] / Suhrkamp Verlag / .

Collation: pp. 200, as follows: Suhrkamp emblem, p. [1]; blank, p. [2]; title page as above, p. [3]; selected information from verso as follows: Erstes bis drittes Tausend: 1968 / , p. [4]; dedication, p. [5]; blank, p. [6]; text, pp. [7]-[8], 9-196, [197]; blank, pp. [198]-[200].

Binding and description: 19 x 11.4 cms. Purple cloth over boards. White strip on top two thirds of spine. Spine is printed in purple on this strip and reads B-T as follows: Donald Barthelme Schneewittchen / . Willy Fleckhaus designed the dust jacket. It is printed in red, black and purple on white. Issued at 17 DM. White end papers. All edges trimmed.

Printing History: One printing, 1968, 3,100 copies,

AB7   *Gallimard edition 1969.*

DONALD   BARTHELME / Blanche-Neige / TRADUIT   DE
L'ANGLAIS / PAR CÉLINE ZINS / [in italics] nrf / GALLIMARD / .

Collation: pp. 216, as follows: blank, pp. [1]-[2]; DU MONDE EN TIER / , p. [3]; blank, p. [4]; title page as above, p. [5]; selected information from verso as follows: © Editions Gallimard, 1969, pur la traduction francaise. / , p. [6]; dedication, p. [7]; blank, p. [8]; text, pp. [9]-[10], 11-212; printing and copyright information, p. [213]; blank, pp. [214]-[216].

Binding and description: 18.6 x 11.5 cms. Paper wraps. Printed in black and red. Spine reads T-B as follows: [all lines printed horizontal] du monde / entier / DONALD / BARTHELME / BLANCHE- / NEIGE / nrf / GALLIMARD / . Issued at 15 FF. All edges untrimmed.

AB8   *Bompiani edition 1972.*

DONALD BARTHELME / Biancaneve / Bompiani / .

Collation: pp. 208, as follows: half title, p. [1]; list of other titles by author published by Bompiani, p. [2]; title page as above, p. [3]; selected information from verso as follows: Traduzione dall' Americano di / GIANCARLO BONACINA/ ©1972 / , p. [4]; dedication, p. [5]; blank, p. [6]; text, pp. [7]-[8], 9-199, [200]; blank, p. [201]; list of other Bompiani titles, pp. [202]-[205]; blank, p. [206]; publishing information, p. [207]; blank, p. [208].

Binding and description: White paper wraps. Printed in blue, black and purple. Spine reads T-B as follows: DONALD BARTHELME / [parallel and below prior line] BIANCANEVE / BOMPIANI / . Issued at 2,000 Lire. All edges trimmed.

AB9   *Meulenhoff edition 1973.*

Donald Barthelme / Sneeuwwitje / Vertaald door Else Hoog / Meulenhoff Amsterdam / Meulenhoffreeks / .

Collation: pp. 152, as follows: half title, p. [1]; blank, p. [2]; title page as above, p. [3]; selected information from verso as follows: Copyright Nederlandse vertaling © 1973 ... / ISBN: 90 290 0233 6 / , p. 4; text, pp. [5]-[6], 7-150, [151]; blank, p. [152].

Binding and description: 20 x 11.3 cms. Decorated wraps. Black lettering on a salmon background. Spine printed in black and reads T-B as follows: Donald Barthelme Sneeuwwitje meulenhoffreeks / (H) mr26 / . Issued at 10 Dfl.

Printing History: One printing, 1973, 5,000 copies.

AB10   *Karisto edition 1973.*

Donald Barthelme / Lumikki / ARVI A. KARISTO OSAKEYH TIÖ / .

Collation: pp. 152, as follows: half title, p. [1]; list of other books by author, p. [2]; title page as above, p. [3]; selected information from verso as follows: Snow White / Suomentanut Liisa Hollmén-Steffa / ISBN 951-23-0700-6 / Arvi A. Karisto / Hämeenlinna 1973 / , p. [4]; dedication, p. [5]; blank, p. [6]; text, pp. [7]-[8], 9-148, [149]; blank, pp. [150]-[152].

Binding and description: 20.5 x 13.2 cms. Red cloth over boards. Spine printed in gold and reads T-B as follows: Donald Barthelme [dot] Lumikki / . Kyllikki Louhivaara designed the dust jacket. Price not determined. White end papers. All edges trimmed.

AC   **UNSPEAKABLE PRACTICES**
          UNNATURAL ACTS

AC1   *First Edition 1968.*

Unspeakable / Practices, / Unnatural Acts / FARRAR, STRAUS AND GIROUX; NEW YORK / [Farrar emblem] / .

Collation: 6 leaves + 172 pp. as follows: blank leaf; half title;verso blank; title page as above; selected information from verso as follows: First printing, 1968 / Design: Jane Bierhorst / ; dedication; verso blank; Contents; verso blank; fly title; verso blank; text, pp. [1]-[2], 3-170; blank, pp. [171]-[172].

Contents: The Indian Uprising / The Balloon / This Newspaper Here / Robert Kennedy Saved From Drowning / Report / The Dolt / The Police Band / Edward and Pia / A Few Moments of

Sleeping and Waking / Can We Talk / Game / Alice / A Picture History Of The War / The President / See the Moon? / .

Binding and description: 20.3 x 13.4 cms. Black cloth over boards. Spine reads T-B as follows: Unspeakable Practices, / [parallel and below first line] Unnatural Acts / [Farrar emblem] FARRAR • STRAUS • GIROUX / [parallel and below prior line] Barthelme / .Title printed in green, balance in orange. Janet Halverson designed the dust jacket which is printed in three colors. Issued at $4.95. Green wove end papers. All edges trimmed. Top edge stained orange.

*Printing History:*First printing, February 9, 1968, 6,500 copies; second printing, June 12, 1973, 1,000 copies.

Note: Mr. Barthelme recalls that bound galleys were distributed in advance of the finished book.

AC2　　　*Bantam edition 1969.*

UNSPEAKABLE / PRACTICES / UNNATURAL / ACTS / [ruled line] / DONALD BARTHELME / [Bantam Emblem] / .

Collation: pp. 4 leaves + 168, as follows: quotes from reviews, 1st leaf + recto of second: list of other titles by author; title page as above; selected information from verso as follows: To Herman Gollob / A Bantam Book [slash] published by arrangement with / Farrar, Straus and Giroux / PRINTING HISTORY / Bantam edition published May 1969 / ; recto of 4th leaf, Contents; verso; blank; text, pp. [1]-[2], 3-165; about the author, p. [166]; ads for other Bantam titles, p. [167]; ad for Bantam catalog, p. [168].

Contents: Identical to first edition.

Binding and description: 17.8 x 10.8 cms. Decorated wraps. Printed in brown, green, red and white. Spine printed in white and reads T-B as follows: [Bantam emblem] / UNSPEAKABLE PRACTICES, / [parallel and below prior line] UNNATURAL ACTS / (H) Donald / (H) Barthelme / 553 • 04411 • 0951 / . Issued at 95¢. All edges trimmed and stained yellow.

Printing History: First printing, April 1969, 113,000 copies; second printing, February 1971, 16,000 copies; third printing, February 1972, 16,000 copies.

AC3   *Pocket Book edition 1976.*

Unspeakable / Practices, / Unnatural Acts / DONALD BARTHELME / PUBLISHED BY POCKET [Pocket Book emblem] BOOKS NEW YORK / .

Collation: 176 pp., as follows: quotes from reviews of first edition, p. [1]; list of other titles by author, p. [2]; title page as above, p. [3]; selected information from verso as follows: POCKET BOOK edition published November 1976 / ISBN 0-671-80771-4. / , p. [4]; dedication, p. [5]; blank, p. [6]; Contents, p. [7]; blank, p. [8]; text, pp. [9], 10-173; ads for other POCKET BOOK titles, pp. [174]-[176].

Contents: Identical to first edition.

Binding and description: 17.8 x 10.5 cms. Decorated paper wraps printed in six colors. Spine is printed in black except for title and reads T-B as follows: (H) [Pocket Book emblem] / (H) POCKET / (H) BOOKS / [in blue-green] UNSPEAKABLE PRACTICES, UNNATURAL ACTS / Donald Barthelme / (H) 0-671 / (H) 80771 / (H) 4-195 / . Issued at $1.95. All edges trimmed and stained yellow.

Printing History: First printing, November 1976, 30,000 copies.

AC4   *Cape edition 1969.*

DONALD BARTHELME / Unspeakable / Practices, / Unnatural Acts / [Cape emblem] / Jonathan Cape Thirty Bedford Square London / .

Collation: 6 leaves + 172, as follows: blank leaf; half title; list of other books by author; title page as above; selected information from verso as follows: This collection first published in Great Britain 1969 / Jonathan Cape Ltd, 30 Bedford Square, London wcl / ; dedication; verso blank; Contents; verso blank; fly title; verso blank; text, pp. [1]-[2], 3-170; blank, pp. [171]-[172].

Contents: Identical to first edition.

Binding and description: 18.7 x 12.4 cms. Purple paper over boards. Spine reads B-T as follows: (H) [Cape Emblem] / Unspeakable Practices, Unnatural Acts [diamond] D. BARTHELME / . Stanley Chapman designed the dust jacket which is printed in purple and black. Issued at £1.25. White end papers. All edges trimmed.

Printing History: One printing, 1969, 2,000 copies.

AC5   *Suhrkamp edition 1969.*

Donald Barthelme [in italics] / Unsägliche Praktiken, / unnatürliche Akte / Erzählungen / Suhrkamp / .

Collation: pp. 196, as follows: [Suhrkamp emblem], p. [1]; blank, p. [2]; title page as above, p. [3]; selected information from verso as follows: Aus dem Amerikanischen . . . Hanna und Adolf Muschg / Erstes bis drittes Tausend 1969 / , p. [4]; dedication, p. [5]; blank, p. [6]; Contents, p. [7]-[8]; text, pp. [9]-[10], 11-195, [196].

Contents: Der Indianeraufstand / Der Ballon / Diese Zeitung hier / Robert Kennedy vor dem Ertrinken gerettet / Report / Der Tropf / Die Polizeikapelle / Edward und Pia / Ein paar Augenblicke Schlafen und Wachen / Können wir reden / Spiel / Alice / Eine Bildergeschichte des Krieges / Der Präsident / Siehst du den Mond? / .

Binding and description: 19.2 x 11.4 cms. Blue cloth over boards. Purple paper label on top one third of spine. Spine printed in three parallel lines on this label and they read B-T as follows: Donald Barthelme [in black] / Unsägliche Praktiken [this line and next printed in white] / Unnatürliche Akte / . Dust jacket is white printed over in purple and black. It was designed by Willy Fleckhaus. Issued at 4.80 DM. White end papers. All edges trimmed.

Printing History: One printing, 1969, 2,100 copies.

AC6   *Bompiani edition 1969.*

DONALD BARTHELME / Atti innaturali, / pratiche innominabili / Bompiani / .

Collation: pp. 160, as follows: half title, p. [1]; list of other Bompiani titles by author, p. [2]; title page as above, p. [3]; selected information from verso as follows: Traduzione di: / RANIERI CARANO / , p. [4]; dedication, p. [5]; blank, p. [6]; text, pp. 7-153; blank, p. [154]; Contents, p. [155]; list of other Bompiani titles, pp. [156]-[159]; publication information, p. [160].

Contents: La rivolta degli indiani / Il pallone / Questo giornale qui / Robert Kennedy salvato dalle acque / Relazione / Il testone / La banda della polizia / Edward e Pia / Qualche momento di sonno e di veglia / Parliamo pure / Partita / Alice / Storia fotografica della guerra / Il presidente / La vedi la luna? / .

Binding and description: 20.5 x 11.7 cms. Decorated paper wraps. Printed in black, yellow and red on white. Spine printed in black and reads T-B as follows: D. BARTHELME / ATTI INNATURALI, PRATICHE INNOMINABILI BOMPIANI /. Issued at 1,500 Lire. All edges trimmed.

AC7   *Bonnier edition 1970.*

Sant Talar Man Tystom, Sånt År Mot Naturen. Translated by Ingmar Forsstrom. Stockholm, Bonnier, 1970. Pp. 140. Issued at 22.50 SwCr.

AC8   *A. A. Karisto edition 1971.*

Donald Barthelme / Mahdottomia tapoja, / luonnottomia tekoja / Suomentanut Juhani Jaskari / ARVI A. KARISTO OSAKEYHTÖ /

Collation: pp. 124, as follows: half title, p. [1]; list of other books by publisher, p. [2]; title page as above, p. [3]; selected information from verso as follows: All rights reserved / Hämeenlinna 1971 / Arvi A. Karisto Oy:n kirjapaino / , p. [4]; dedication, p. [5]; blank, p. [6]; Contents, p. [7]; blank, p. [8]; text, pp. [9]-[10], 11-121; blank, [122]-[124].

Contents: Kupla / Robert Kennedy pelastuu hukkumasta / Raportti / Tomppeli / Edward ja Piä / Muutama hetki unta ja valvetta / Voimmeko puhua / Pelia / Presidentti / Sodan historia kuvina / .

Binding and description: 18 x 11.1 cms. Decorated wraps. Printed in five colors. Spine reads T-B as follows: BARTHELME [dot] MAHDOTTOMIA TAPOJA [parallel and below preceding line] LUONNOTTOMIA TEKOIA / . Issued at 11 Markka. All edges trimmed.

AC9   *Editorial Anagrama edition 1972.*

Donald Barthelme / Prácticas indecibles, / actos antinaturales / [publisher's emblem] / EDITORIAL ANAGRAMA / BARCELONA / .

Collation: pp.176, as follows: half title, p. [1]; blank, p. [2]; title page as above, p. [3]; selected information from verso as follows: Traducción: / José Manuel Alvarez y Ángela Perez / © EDITORIAL

ANAGRAMA / , p. [4]; dedication, p. [5]; blank, p. [6]; text, pp. [7]-[8], 9-173; blank, p. [174]; Contents, p. [175]; list of other title by publisher in SERIE INFORMAL, p. [176].

Contents: La revuelta india / El globo / Este periódico que tengo aquí / Robert Kennedy salvado de las aguas / Informe / El zopenco / La banda de la policía / Edward y Pia / Algunos momentos de sueno y de vigilia / Podemos hablar / Juego / Alicia / Historia ilustrade de la guerra / El Presidente / ¿Ves la luna? / .

Binding and description: 20 x 12.8 cms. Decorated paper wraps. Printed in blue and greenish blue. Spine printed in white and reads B-T as follows: [publisher's emblem] Barthelme / [in italics] Prácticas indecibles actos antinaturales / . Issued at 170 pts. All edges trimmed.

AC10   *Gyldendal edition 1972.*

DONALD BARTHELME / En regn af guld of / andre noveller / PÅ DANSK VED / ARNE HERLØV PETERSEN / GYLDENDAL / .

Collation: pp. 180, as follows: half title, p. [1]; blank, p. [2]; title page as above, p. [3]; selected information from verso as follows: Printed in Denmark 1972. / ISBN 87 00 21331 4 / , p. [4]; Contents, p. [5]; blank, p. [6]; text, pp. 7-177; blank, pp. [178]-[180].

Contents: Indianeropstanden / Ballonen / Robert Kennedy reddet fra at drukne / Rapport / Fjolset / Politiorkestret / Edward og Pia / Nogle øjeblikke vågen og sovende / Praesidenten / Har du set månen? / Florence Green er 81 / Vil du fortaelle mig det? / For jeg er den fyr, hvis eneste glaede det er at elske dig / Den store radiodsendelse 1938 / Marie, Marie, haeng endelig ved / Op at flyve i luften / Til London og Rom / En regn af guld / .

Binding and description: 21 x 12.8 cms. Decorated wraps printed in yellow and black. Spine reads T-B as follows: DONALD BARTHELME [in white] EN REGNE AF GULD [in yellow] GYLDENDAL [in white]. Issued at 23 DAN. KR. All edges untrimmed.

Printing History: One printing, March 10, 1972, 3,000 copies.

Note: This book contains stories from both *Unspeakable Practices, Unnatural Acts* and *Come Back, Dr. Caligari*.

AC11   *Gallimard edition 1972.*

DONALD BARTHELME / Pratiques / innommables / TRADUIT DE L'ANGLAIS / PAR CÉLINE ZINS / [in italics] nrf / GALLIMARD /.

Collation: pp. 288, as follows: blank, pp. [1]-[2]; DU MONDE EN TIER / , p. [3]; blank, p. [4]; title page as above, p. [5]; selected information from verso as follows: Les nouvelles composant ce recueil sont extraites de: / [in italics] Come back, Dr. Caligari ... / [in italics] Unspeakable practices, unnatural acts ... / © Éditions Gallimard, 1972, pour la traduction française. / , p. [6]; text pp. [7]-[9], 10-182; Contents, p. [283]; blank, p. [284]; By same author, p. [285]; blank, p. [286]; printing information, p. [287]; blank, p. [288].

Contents: Les quartre-vingt-un ans de Florence Green / Le pianiste / Me direz-vous? / Car le gars dont la seule joie est de t'aimer c'est moi / La grande emission de 1938 / Marie, Marie, cramponne-toi / Tout en haut dans l'air / Marges / Le voyage à Londres et à Rome / Une pluie d'Or / L'insurrection des Indiens / Le ballon / Robert Kennedy sauvé des eaux / Le nigaud / L'orchestre de police / Edouard et Pia / Quelques moments de sommeil et de réveil / Le Président / Tu vois la lune? / .

Binding and description: 20.5 x 14 cms. Paper wraps. Printed in black and red. Spine reads T-B as follows: [all lines horizontal] du monde / entier / DONALD / BARTHELME / PRATIQUES / IN NOMMABLES / [in italics] nrf / GALLIMARD / . Issued at 27 FF. All edges trimmed.

Note: This volume contains stories from both *Come Back, Dr. Caligari* and *Unspeakable Practices, Unnatural Acts.*

AD   CITY LIFE

AD1   *First edition 1970.*

City Life / Donald Barthelme / [Farrar Emblem] / Farrar, Straus & Giroux New York / .

Collation: pp. 4 leaves + 168, as follows: half title; list of other titles by author; title page as above; selected information from verso as follows: Published simultaneously in Canada / by Doubleday

Canada Ltd., Toronto / First printing, 1970 / Designed by Patricia de Groot / ; dedication; blank; contents; blank; text, pp. [1]-[2], 3-168.

Contents: Views of My Father Weeping / Paraguay / The Falling Dog / At the Tolstoy Museum / The Policemen's Ball / The Glass Mountain / The Explantion / Kierkegaard Unfair to Schlegel / The Phantom of the Opera's Friend / Sentence / Bone Bubbles / On Angels / Brain Damage / City Life / .

Binding and description: 21.6 x 15.7 cms. Red cloth over boards. Spine printed in black and reads T-B as follows: City Life / Donald Barthelme / (H) Farrar, / (H) Straus & / (H) Giroux / [Farrar Emblem] / . Dust jacket is orange printed in red, black and white. Black free end papers. Issued at $5.95. All edges trimmed. Top edge stained orange.

Printing History: First printing, March 17, 1970, 6,500 copies; second printing, May 20, 1970, 4,000 copies; third printing, March 17, 1975, 1,000 copies.

Note: Farrar, Straus and Giroux report that approximately twenty sets of bound galleys were distributed in advance of publication.

AD2   *Bantam edition 1971.*

CITY / LIFE / DONALD BARTHELME / [Bantam Emblem] / A NATIONAL GENERAL COMPANY / .

Collation: pp. 5 leaves + 182, as follows: quote from review by Jack Kroll; list of other titles by author; title page as above; selected information from verso as follows: A Bantam Book / Bantam edition published May 1971 / ; dedication; blank; Contents; blank; fly title; blank; text, pp. [1]-[2], 3-180; blank, [181]; "About the author" statement, p. [182].

Contents: Identical to first edition.

Binding and description: 17.8 x 10.7 cms. Decorated wraps. Printed in green, black and white. Spine reads as follows: [(H) - Bantam Emblem] / CITY LIFE / DONALD / [parallel and below first name] BARTHELME / (H) 05908 / (H) 125 / . Issued at $1.25. All edges trimmed and stained yellow.

Printing History: One printing, April 1971, 110,000 copies.

AD3   *Pocket Book edition 1976.*

City Life / Donald Barthelme / PUBLISHED BY POCKET [Pocket Book emblem] BOOKS NEW YORK / .

> *Collation:* pp. 176, as follows: quotes from reviews about the author, p. [1]; list of other titles by author, p. [2]; title page as above, p. [3]; selected information from verso as follows: POCKET BOOK edition published November, 1976 / ISBN 0-671-80770-6. / , p. [4]; dedication, p. [5]; blank, p. [6]; Contents, p. [7]; blank, p. [8]; fly title, p. [9]; blank, p. [10]; text, pp. 11-173; ads for other POCKET BOOKS, pp. [174]-[176].
>
> *Contents:* Identical to first edition.
>
> *Binding and description:* 17.8 x 10.5 cms. Decorated paper wraps printed in five colors. Spine printed in black except for title and reads T-B as follows: (H) [Pocket Book emblem] / (H)POCKET / (H) BOOKS / (H)FICTION / [in purple] CITY LIFE / Donald Barthelme 0-671-80770-195 / . Issued at $1.95. All edges trimmed and stained yellow.
>
> *Printing History:* First printing, November 1976, 30,000 copies.

AD4   *Cape edition 1971.*

City Life / Donald Barthelme / [Cape emblem] / Jonathan Cape Thirty Bedford Square London / .

> *Collation:* pp. 4 leaves + 168, as follows: half title; list of other titles by author; title page as above; selected information from verso as follows: First published in Great Britain 1971 / ; dedication; verso blank; Contents; verso blank; text, pp. [1]-[2], 3-168.
>
> *Contents:* See listing for first edition.
>
> *Binding and description:* 19.7 x 12.3 cms. Brown paper over boards. Spine printed in gold and reads T-B as follows: CITY LIFE DONALD BARTHELME / (H)[Cape emblem] / . Stanley Chapman designed the dust jacket which is printed in black, blue and green. Issued at £1.50. White end papers. All edges trimmed. Top edge stained blue.
>
> *Printing History:* One printing, 1971, 2,000 copies.

AD5   *Suhrkamp edition 1972.*

Donald Barthelme / City Life / [in italics] Erzählungen / Suhrkamp Verlag / .

Collation: pp. 200, as follows: Suhrkamp series identification, p. [1]; blank, p. [2]; title page as above, p. [3]; selected information from verso as follows: Erste Auflage 1972 / Deutsch von Marianne Oellers / , p. [4]; Contents, p. [5]; dedication, p. [6]; text, pp. [7]-[8], 9-196, [197]; blank, p. [198]; list of other Suhrkamp titles, pp. [199]-[200].

Contents: Meinen Vater weinen sehen / Paraguay / Der fallende Hund / Im Tolstoi-Museum / Der Polizistenball / Der Glasberg / Die Erläuterung / Kierkegaard gegenuber Schlegel unfair / Freund des Phantoms der Oper / Satz / Knochenblasen / Über Engel / Hirnschaden / City Life / .

Binding and description: 18 x 11 cms. Blue paper over boards. Top part of spine has a white printed label area on which the author and title are printed in gold. It is printed parallel to the spine and reads B-T as follows: DONALD BARTHELME [parallel and below prior line] CITY LIFE / . Willy Fleckhaus designed the dust jacket. It is printed in black and blue. Issued at 8.80 DM. White end papers. All edges trimmed.

Printing History: One printing, 1972, 3,600 copies.

AD6   *Editorial Anagrama edition 1974.*

Donald Barthelme / City Life / [publisher's emblem] / EDITORIAL ANAGRAMA / BARCELONA / .

Collation: pp. 160, as follows: half title, p. [1]; blank, p. [2]; title page as above, p. [3]; selected information from verso as follows: Traducción / José Manuel y Ángel Pérez / © EDITORIAL ANAGRAMA / ISBN 84-3393-317-9 / , p. [4]; text, pp. [5]-[6], 7-158; Contents, p. [159]; list of other titles in SERIE INFORMAL, p. [160].

Contents: Escenas de mi padre llorando / Paraguay / Perro cayendo / En el museo Tolstoi / El baile de los policías / La montaña de cristal / La explicación / Kierkegaard es injusto con Schlegel / El amigo del fantasma de la ópera / Frase / Burbujas óseas / Sobre los ángeles / Lesión cerebral / City Life / .

Binding and description: 20 x 13.1 cms. Decorated paper wraps. Printed in orange and green over white and lettering shows through as white. Spine reads B-T as follows: [publisher's emblem] Barthelme / [in italics] City Life / . Issued at 170 pts. All edges trimmed.

AD7   *Norstedt edition 1972.*

DONALD BARTHELME / STORSTADSLIV / Översättning av Gunnar Barklund / P. A. Norstedt & Söners Förlag / Stockholm / .

Collation: pp. 168, as follows: brief biographical sketch, p. [1]; blank, p. [2]; title page as above, p. [3]; selected information from verso as follows: ISBN 91-1-725751-4 / , p. [4]; dedication, p. [5]; blank, p. [6]; Contents, p. [7]; blank, p. [8]; text, pp. [9]-[10], 11-158, [159]; ads for other books in series, pp. [160]-[168].

Contents: Bilder av min far, gråtande / Paraguay / Den fallande hunden / I Tolstojmuseet / Polisernas bal / Glasberget / Förklaringen / Kierkegaard orättvis mot Schlegal / En vän till Fantomen på Operan / Mening / Benbubblor / Om änglar / Hjärnskada / Storstadsliv / .

Binding and description: 18.9 x 11.2 cms. Decorated wraps printed in black, orange, yellow and purple over white. Spine reads T-B as follows: BARTHELME [in white letters] / Storstadsliv [title in black] / . Issued at 27 Sw. crs. All edges trimmed.

Printing History: One printing, October 30, 1972, 2,200 copies.

AE   THE SLIGHTLY IRREGULAR FIRE ENGINE

AE1   *First edition 1971.*

Donald Barthelme / [following two lines in green] THE SLIGHTLY IRREGULAR / FIRE ENGINE / or The Hithering Thithering Djinn / [green hand, with index finger extended, points to beginning of next line] Copyright © 1971 by Donald Barthelme. All rights reserved. Library of Congress catalog card number: 70-162793. SBN 374.3.7038.9. Published simultaneously in Canada by / Doubleday Canada Ltd., Toronto. Printed in the United States of America. First edition, 1971. / .

Collation: 32 pp. all unnumbered, as follows: dedication, p. [1]; illus., p. [2]; title page as above, p. [3]; story, pp. [4]-[31]; printing information, p. [32].

Binding and description: 28 x 12.4 cms. Green cloth over boards. Spine reads T-B as follows: DONALD BARTHELME / THE SLIGHTLY IRREGULAR FIRE ENGINE / F.S • G / . Author's name and publisher's initials are in red, the title in black. Jacket typography by Jane Bierhorst. Jacket designed by Donald Barthelme. Issued at $4.95. Black end papers. All edges trimmed.

Printing History: First printing, June 17, 1971, 13,000 copies.

AF SADNESS

AF1 *First edition 1972.*

SADNESS / Donald Barthelme / [Farrar emblem] / FARRAR, STRAUS AND GIROUX / NEW YORK / .

Collation: pp. 4 leaves + 184, as follows: half title; list of other books by author; title page as above; selected information from verso as follows: First printing, 1972 / ISBN 0-374-25333-I / ; dedication; verso blank; Contents; verso blank; text, pp. [1]-[2], 3-183; blank, p. [184].

Contents: Critique de la Vie Quotidienne / Traumerei / The Genius / Perpetua / A City of Churches / The Party / Engineer-Private Paul Klee Misplaces an Aircraft Between Milbertshofen and Cambrai, March 1916 / A Film / The Sandman / Departures / Subpeona / The Catechist / The Flight of Pigeons from the Palace / The Rise of Capitalism / The Temptation of St. Anthony / Daumier / .

Binding and description: 21.5 x 15.5 cms. Purple cloth over boards. Spine printed in silver and reads T-B as follows: Barthelme SADNESS Farrar Straus Giroux / . Dust jacket designed by author. Grey end papers. Issued at $5.95. All edges trimmed. Top edge stained green.

Printing History: First printing, September 19, 1972, 9,900 copies; second printing, September 13, 1973, 1,000 copies.

Note: Approximately twenty sets of galleys, set before page proofs and bound in tall green paper wrappers, were distributed in advance of publication. The order of stories varies considerably from the finished edition: Critique de la Vie Quotidienne, The Temptation of St. Anthony, The Party, A City of Churches, Subpoena, Perpetua, A Film, The Catechist, Departures, The Sandman, The Flight of Pigeons from the Palace, The Genius, Engineer-Private Paul Klee..., The Rise of Capitalism, Traumerei, Daumier.

AF2 *Bantam edition 1974.*

SADNESS / Donald Barthelme / [Bantam Emblem] / .

Collation: pp. 4 leaves + 184, as follows: quotations from two reviews; list of other titles by author; title page as above; selected information from verso as follows: A Bantam Book / Bantam edition published November 1974 / ; Contents; verso blank; dedication; verso blank; text, pp. [1]-[2], 3-181; "About the Author" statement, p. [182]; ads for other Bantam titles, pp. [183]-[184].

Contents: Identical to first edition.

Binding and description: 18 x 10.5 cms. Decorated wraps printed in five colors. Spine printed in black save publisher's emblem which is in black and red and reads T-B as follows: (H) [publisher's emblem] / (H) Liter- / (H) ature / (H) [ruled line] / (H) [ruled line] / (H) $1.65 / SADNESS DONALD BARTHELME / (H) 553 / (H) 07824 / (H) 165 / . Issued at $1.65. All edges trimmed.

Printing History: First printing, October 1974, 39,000 copies; second printing, March 1975, 25,000 copies.

AF3 *Cape edition 1973.*

Donald Barthelme / [ruled line] / SADNESS / [Cape emblem] / JONATHAN CAPE / THIRTY BEDFORD SQUARE LONDON / .

Collation: pp. 4 leaves + 184, as follows: half title; list of other titles by author; title page as above; selected information from verso as follows: FIRST PUBLISHED IN GREAT BRITAIN 1973 / JONATHAN CAPE LTD, / ISBN 0 224 00897 8 / ; Contents; verso blank; dedication; verso blank; text, pp. [1]-[2], 3-183; blank, p. [184].

Contents: Identical to first edition

Binding and description: 20.9 x 14.5 cms. Red paper over boards. Spine printed in gold and reads T-B as follows: SADNESS DONALD BARTHELME / [Cape emblem] / . Keith Davis designed the dust jacket which is brown and printed over in red and black. Issued at $12.50. White end papers. All edges trimmed.

Printing History: One printing, 1973, 2,000 copies.

AG   GUILTY PLEASURES

AG1   *First edition 1974.*

Guilty / Pleasures / DONALD BARTHELME / Farrar, Straus and Giroux • New York [Farrar emblem] / .

Collation: pp. 5 leaves + 166, as follows: half title; list of other titles by author; title page as above; selected information from verso as follows: First printing, 1974 /; dedication; verso blank; author's comment; verso blank; Contents, recto and verso of fifth leaf; text, pp. [1]-[2], 3-165; blank, p. [166].

Contents: [the stories are divided into three groups] ONE / Down the Line with the Annual / Letters to the Editore / That Cosmopolitan Girl / Eugénie Grandet / Snap Snap / The Angry Young Man / L'Lapse / The Teachings of Don B.: A Yankee Way of Knowledge / TWO / Swallowing / The Yound Visitirs / The Palace / The Dragon / An Hesitation on the Bank of the Delaware / The Royal Treatment / Mr. Foolfarm's Journal / THREE / Heliotrope / And Now Let's Hear It for the Ed Sullivan Show! / Bunny Image, Loss of: The Case of Bitsy S. / The Expedition / Games Are the Enemies of Beauty, Truth, and Sleep, Amanda Said / A Nation of Wheels / Two Hours to Curtain / The Photographs / Nothing: A Preliminary Account / .

Binding and description: 21.4 x 15.4 cms. Yellow cloth over boards. Spine printed in black and reads T-B as follows: DONALD BARTHELME / Guilty Pleasures / [parallel and below Pleasures] FARRAR STRAUS GIROUX / . Dust jacket designed by author. Issued at $7.95. White end papers. All edges trimmed.

Printing History: One printing, September 11, 1974, 10,000 copies.

Note: Approximately twenty sets of galleys, page proofs bound in green paper wrappers, were distributed in advance of publication.

AG2   *Delta Re-edition of first edition 1976.*

Guilty Pleasures / DONALD BARTHELME/ [Delta emblem] / A DELTA BOOK / .

Collation: pp. 8 leaves + 166, as follows: list of titles of related interest published by Delta; verso blank; title page as above; selected information from verso as follows: First Delta printing - February

1976 / ; dedication; verso blank; author's comment on the stories; verso blank; Contents; verso has conclusion of Contents; text, pp. [1]-[2], 3-164, [165]; blank, p. [166].

Contents: See listing for first edition.

Binding and description: 19.4 x 13.5 cms. Decorated wraps. Printed in black, pink and yellow. Spine reads T-B as follows: [Delta emblem] / Guilty Pleasures Donald Barthelme 440-04782-265 / . Issued at $2.65. All edges trimmed.

Printing History: First printing, February 1976, 7,500 copies; second printing, February 1976, 7,500 copies.

AH THE DEAD FATHER

AH1 *First edition 1975.*

The Dead Father / DONALD BARTHELME / [Farrar emblem] NEW YORK / FARRAR, STRAUS AND GIROUX / .

Collation: pp. 5 leaves + 178 + 2 leaves, as follows: blank leaf; fly title; verso blank; list of other works by author; verso blank; title page as above; selected information from verso as follows: Copyright © BY Donald Barthelme / First printing, 1975 / ; dedication; verso blank; text, pp. [1]-[2], 3-177, [178]; two blank leaves.

Binding and description: 20.2 x 13.5 cms. Black cloth over boards. Spine is printed in silver and reads T-B as follows: DONALD BARTHELME / (H) FARRAR / (H) STRAUS / (H) GIROUX / THE DEAD FATHER / . Ruth Ansel designed the dust jacket which is silver and printed in black. Gray end papers. Issued at $7.95. All edges trimmed.

Printing History: One printing, 1975, 12,000 copies.

Note: This volume was not issued with signatures which are sewn, but has the cut and glued binding sometimes called "perfect binding."

Note 2: Approximately twenty sets of galleys, page proofs bound in red paper wrappers, were distributed in advance of publication.

Note 3: A self contained section of *The Dead Father*, "A Manual For Sons," was published in the *New Yorker*, 42 (May 12, 1975), pp. 40-50 as "Manual for Sons" with two sections placed in a different order and with other minor changes.

AH2 *Pocket Book edition 1976.*

The Dead Father / Donald Barthelme / PUBLISHED BY POCKET [Publisher's emblem] BOOKS NEW YORK / .

Collation: pp. 224, as follows: quotes from reviews of hardcover printing, p. [1]; list of other books by author, p. [2]; title page as above, p. [3]; selected information from verso as follows: POCKET BOOK edition published November, 1976 / ISBN 0-671-80766-8. / , p. [4]; dedication, p. [5]; blank, p. [6]; fly title, p. [7]; blank, p. [8]; text, pp. 9-220; ads for other Pocket Book titles, pp. [221]-[224].

Binding and description: 17.8 x 10.5 cms. Decorated paper wraps printed in seven colors. Spine printed in black except for title and reads T-B as follows: (H) [Publisher's emblem] / (H) POCKET / (H) BOOKS / (H) FICTION / [in red] THE DEAD FATHER / Donald Barthelme 0.671.80766.8.195 / . Issued at $1.95. All edges trimmed and stained yellow.

Printing History: First printing. November 1976, 80,000 copies.

AI AMATEURS

AI1 *First edition 1976.*

AMATEURS / Donald Barthelme / [Farrar emblem] / FARRAR, STRAUS AND GIROUX / NEW YORK / .

Collation: pp. vii + 184, as follows: Half title, p. [i]; list of other books by author, p. [ii]; title page as above, p. [iii]; selected information from verso as follows: First Printing, 1976 / , p. [iv]; dedication, p. [v]; blank, p. [vi]; Contents, pp. vii-viii; text, pp. [1]-[2], 3-183, [184].

Contents: Our Work and Why We Do It / The Wound / 110 West Sixty-first Street / Some of Us Had Been Threatening [slash] Our Friend Colby / The School / The Great Hug / I Bought a Little City / The Agreement / The Sergeant / What to Do Next / The Captured Woman / And Then / Porcupines at the University / The Educational Experience / The Discovery / Rebecca / The Reference / The New Member / You Are as Brave as Vincent van Gogh / At the End of the Mechanical Age / .

Binding and description: 19.2 x 13.5 cms. Orange cloth over boards. Spine printed in gold and reads T-B as follows: AMATEURS / Barthelme / FARRAR STRAUS GIROUX / . Muriel Nasser designed the dust jacket which is printed in four colors. White end papers. All edges trimmed. Top edge stained black.

Note: Approximately twenty sets of galleys, page proofs bound in grey wrappers, were distributed in advance of publication. The first announcement of this collection indicated "The Death of Edward Lear" would be included, but it was dropped before publication by the author.

B

SHORT STORIES AND FICTIONAL PARODIES

1961

B1   "The Darling Duckling at School." *Contact* no.7 (February), pp. 17-28. Rpt. as "Me and Miss Mandible" in *CB* with minor stylistic changes, including the name "Martha" to "Brenda."

B2   "The Hiding Man." *First Person* 1 (Spring-Summer): 65-75. Rpt. as "Hiding Man" in *CB* with minor stylistic changes.

1962

B3   "The Big Broadcast of 1938." *New World Writing* no.20, pp. 108-120. Rpt. in *CB* with two minor stylistic elisions.

B4   "The Viennese Opera Ball." *Contact* no.10 (June), pp. 40, 42-44. Rpt. in *CB* with several stylistic changes and elisions, including the list of terms beginning with the letter "f" on p. 43.

1963

B5   "L'Lapse." *New Yorker* 39 (March 2): 29-31. Rpt. in *GP* with two stylistic elisions.

B6 "Florence Green is 81." *Harper's Bazaar* 92 (April): 130-131, 200, 209, 217. Rpt. in *CB* with minor stylistic changes.

B7 "The Piano Player." *New Yorker* 39 (August 31): 24. Rpt. in *CB* with minor stylistic changes.

B8 "To London and Rome." *Genesis West* 2 (Fall): 33-38. Rpt. in *CB* with minor stylistic elisions and several minor stylistic changes.

B9 "Marie, Marie, Hold On Tight." *New Yorker* 39 (October 12): 49-51. Rpt. in *CB* with several minor stylistic changes.

B10 "A Shower of Gold." *New Yorker* 39 (December 28): 33-37. Rpt. in *CB* with several minor stylistic changes and elisions.

1964

B11 "Margins." *New Yorker* 40 (February 22): 33-34. Rpt. in *CB* with several minor stylistic changes and elisions.

B12 "Will You Tell Me?" *Art and Literature* no.1 (March), pp. 68-76. Rpt. in *CB* without the number "1" mentioned on p. 68.

B13 "Down the Line With the Annual." *New Yorker* 40 (March 21): 34-35. Rpt. in *GP* with the change of "1958" to "1968" and "nasty, brutish, and short" to "a feeble, flickering thing."

B14 "Man's Face." *New Yorker* 40 (May 30): 29.

B15 "For I'm the Boy." *Location* 1 (Summer): 91-93. Rpt. as "For I'm the Boy Whose Only Joy Is Loving You" in *CB* with minor stylistic changes and additions.

B16 "The Joker's Greatest Triumph." First appearance in *CB*.

B17 "Up, Aloft in the Air." First appearance in *CB*.

B18 "A Picture History of the War." *New Yorker* 40 (June 20): 28-31. Rpt. in *UP* with minor stylistic changes and elisions.

B19 "The Police Band." *New Yorker* 40 (August 22): 28. Rpt. in *UP*.

B20 "The President." *New Yorker* 40 (September 5): 26-27. Rpt. in *UP*.

B21 "Then." *Mother* no.3 (November-December), pp. 22-23.

1965

B22 "The Indian Uprising." *New Yorker* 41 (March 6): 34-37. Rpt. in *UP* with minor stylistic changes.

B23 "Game." *New Yorker* 41 (July 31): 29-30. Rpt. in *UP* with minor stylistic changes and elisions.

B24 "Can We Talk." *Art and Literature* no.5 (Summer), pp. 148-150. Rpt. in *UP* with minor stylistic changes and one small elision.

B25 "Snap Snap." *New Yorker* 41 (August 28): 108, 110-111. Rpt. in *GP* with the change of *"World Business"* to *"Time."*

B26 "Edward and Pia." *New Yorker* 41 (September 25): 46-49. Rpt. in *UP*.

B27 "The Affront." *Harper's Bazaar* 94 (November): 169, 229-230. Rpt. in *SW* with minor stylistic changes and substantial elisions.

1966

B28 "This Newspaper Here." *New Yorker* 41 (February 12): 28-29. Rpt. in *UP* with minor stylistic changes.

B29 "See the Moon?" *New Yorker* 42 (March 12): 46-50. Rpt. in *UP* with minor stylistic changes.

B30 "Several Garlic Tales." *Paris Review* no.37 (Spring), pp. 62-67. Rpt. in *SW* with several substantial additions.

B31 "The Balloon." *New Yorker* 42 (April 16): 46-48. Rpt. in *UP* with minor stylistic changes.

B32 "Games Are the Enemies of Beauty, Truth, and Sleep, Amanda Said." *Mademoiselle* 64 (November): 212-213. Rpt. in *GP* with minor stylistic changes and one elision, following "Barcelona" on p. 213.

1967

B33 "Report." *New Yorker* 43 (June 10): 34-35. Rpt. in *UP*.

B34 "A Few Moments of Sleeping and Waking." *New Yorker* 43 (August 5): 24-26. Rpt. in *UP*.

B35 "The Dolt." *New Yorker* 43 (November 11): 56-58. Rpt. in *UP* with minor stylistic changes and one elision.

1968

B36 "Robert Kennedy Saved From Drowning." *New American Review* no.3 (April 1968), pp. 107-116. Rpt. in *UP* with one minor elision.

B37 "The Explanation." *New Yorker* 44 (May 4): 44-46. Rpt. in *CL* with minor stylistic changes and elisions.

B38 "The Policemen's Ball." *New Yorker* 44 (June 8): 31. Rpt. in *CL* with the change in the automobile's model year from '68 to '70.

B39 "Alice." *Paris Review* no.43 (Summer), pp. 25-31. Rpt. in *UP* with one minor stylistic addition.

B40 "The Falling Dog. *New Yorker* 44 (August 3): 28-29. Rpt. in *CL* with a different order of opening paragraphs and with minor stylistic changes.

B41 "Eugénie Grandet." *New Yorker* 44 (August 17): 24-25. Rpt. in *GP* with "butter" mentioned 87 times instead of 113 times, and with a different photograph of "Charles of the Indies."

B42 "Kierkegaard Unfair to Schlegel." *New Yorker* 44 (October 12): 53-55. Rpt. in *CL* with one small addition.

B43 "Philadelphia." *New Yorker* 44 (November 30): 56-58.

1969

B44 "City Life." *New Yorker* 44 (January 18): 31-32. Rpt. in *CL* as the first half of story with one minor stylistic change.

B45 "City Life II." *New Yorker* 45 (June 21): 32-37. Rpt. in *CL* as second half of story with much rearranging of sections and substantial elisions.

B46 "And Now Let's Hear It for the Ed Sullivan Show!" *Esquire* 71 (April): 126-127, 54, 56. Rpt. in *GP*.

B47 "At the Tolstoy Museum." *New Yorker* 45 (May 24): 32-37. Rpt. in *CL* with minor stylistic changes and minus two pictures.

B48 "On Angels." *New Yorker* 45 (August 9): 29. Rpt. in *CL* with minor stylistic changes.

B49 "Paraguay." *New Yorker* 45 (September 6): 32-34. Rpt. in *CL* with minor stylistic changes.

B50 "Mouth." *Paris Review* no.48 (Fall), pp. 189-202. Rpt. in *CL* as "Bone Bubbles" with many minor stylistic changes and two rearrangements of paragraphs.

B51 "Views of My Father Weeping." *New Yorker* 45 (December 6): 56-60. Rpt. in *CL* with minor stylistic changes and additions.

1970

B52 "The Phantom of the Opera's Friend." *New Yorker* 45 (February 7): 26-27. Rpt. in *CL* with additional paragraphing.

B53 "Brain Damage." *New Yorker* 46 (February 21): 42-43. Rpt. in *CL* with substantial reordering and additions, plus minor stylistic changes.

B54 "Sentence." *New Yorker* 45 (March 7): 34-36. Rpt. in *CL* with minor stylistic changes.

B55 "Porcupines at the University." *New Yorker* 46 (April 25): 32-33. Rpt. in in *A* with one minor stylistic change, plus the changes of "The Ed Sullivan Show" to "The Sonny and Cher Show" and "Mr. Ed Sullivan" to "Mr. Sonny Bono."

B56 "A Nation of Wheels." *New Yorker* 46 (June 13): 36-39. Rpt. in *GP* with paragraphs 4 and 5 reversed.

B57 Untitled, unsigned "Comment" piece, columns 1, 2, and half of 3, *New Yorker* 46 (June 13): 25. Parts subsequently incorporated into "Flying to America" (B76) which in turn became part of "A Film" (B61) in S. (Note: earlier unsigned "Comment" pieces by Barthelme may predate this contribution, the first for which the *New Yorker* kept a record.) The textual history of the book version is the most complex of any Barthelme story. The serial versions of the latter stories are not so much combined as intercut, with "A Film" providing the structure and "Flying to America" much of the texture, including the assistant Ezra and the eponymous sequence which furnishes the climax. Part of "Flying to America" not used in "A Film," the filming of country music (pp. 52-54), was resurrected as "Two Hours to Curtain" in *GP* (see B76). Considerably more—roughly half the original story—has not reappeared in any form. This materia includes the scriptwriters, the genius, the Silverman subplot, the narrator's father, the rebellion of the crew and the film's seizure, the character Perpetua, and the use of the narrator's name, Thomas Rush. Throughout are many minor stylistic changes and additions.

B58 "The Glass Mountain." First Appearance in *CL*.

B59 "Newsletter." *New Yorker* 46 (July 11): 23.

B60 "The Show." *New Yorker* 46 (August 8): 26-29. Rpt. in S as "The Flight of Pigeons from the Palace," with several variations in number and order and number of illustrations, and with segments beginning "Performances flew" and "I put my father" (pp. 136-137) in reverse order. One minor addition on pp. 138-139 adds the title of the story and changes "monster" to "cacodemon."

B61 "A Film." *New Yorker* 46 (September 26): 31. See B57. Rpt. in S.

B62 "Adventure." *Harper's Bazaar* 104 (December): 92-95.

B63 "The Rise of Capitalism." *New Yorker* 46 (December 12): 45-47. Rpt. in S, with dots separating segments instead of numbers.

1971

B64 "The Death of Edward Lear." *New Yorker* 46 (January 2): 21. This story was first announced as being reprinted in *A*, but was removed by the author before galleys and publication.

B65 "The Genius." *New Yorker* 47 (February 20): 38-40. Rpt. in *S* with minor stylistic changes and the change of "Thomas Aquinas" to "the Venerable Bede."

B66 "Engineer-Private Paul Klee Misplaces an Aircraft Between Milbertshofen and Cambrai, March 1916." *New Yorker* 47 (April 3): 33-34. Rpt. in *S* with one change of tense on p. 67.

B67 "The Story Thus Far:" *New Yorker* 47 (May 1): 42-45.

B68 "Subpoena." *New Yorker* 47 (May 29): 33. Rpt. in *S* with minor stylistic additions and the change of "J & B" to "whiskey" on p. 115.

B69 "Perpetua." *New Yorker* 47 (June 12) 40-42. Rpt. in *S* with minor stylistic changes.

B70 "Critique de la Vie Quotidienne." *New Yorker* 47 (July 17): 26-29. Rpt. in *S* with "take a flying fuck at the moon" restored in place of dashes.

B71 "Natural History." *Harper's* 243 (August): 44-45.

B72 "The Mothball Fleet." *New Yorker* 47 (September 11): 34-35.

B73 "Departures." *New Yorker* 47 (October 9): 42-44. Rpt. in *S* with minor stylistic changes and an entirely rewritten section 5.

B74 "The Catechist." *New Yorker* 47 (November 13): 49-51. Rpt. in *S* with "General Electric" changed to "General Foods."

B75 "Alexandria and Henrietta." *New American Review* no.12 (December), pp. 82-87.

B76 "Flying to America." *New Yorker* 47 (December 4): 50-58. See B57. Sections not previously reprinted were used in "Two Hours to Curtain" in *GP*, and in *DF*. Several stylistic changes are in evidence.

1972

B77 "The Party." *New Yorker* 48 (February 26): 30-31. Rpt. in S with one minor stylistic change.

B78 Untitled, unsigned "Comment" piece. *New Yorker* 48 (February 26): 25-26. Rpt. in *GP* as "The Dragon," with minor stylistic changes.

B79 "Daumier." *New Yorker* 48 (April 1): 31-36. Rpt. in S with minor stylistic changes.

B80 "A City of Churches." *New Yorker* 48 (April 22): 38-39. Rpt. in S with a minor stylistic change and one small addition.

B81 "The Temptation of St. Anthony." *New Yorker* 48 (June 3): 34-36. Rpt. in S with minor stylistic changes.

B82 "The Expedition." *Audience* 2 (July-August): 56-60. Rpt. in *GP*.

B83 "The Sandman." *Atlantic* 230 (September): 62-65. Rpt. in S with minor stylistic changes.

B84 "Edwards, Amelia." *New Yorker* 48 (September 9): 34-36.

B85 "Traumerei." First appearance in S.

B86 "Three." *Fiction* 1 (no.1): 13.

B87 "Wrack." *New Yorker* 48 (October 21): 36-37.

B88 "Swallowing." *New York Times* November 4, p. 33. Rpt. in *GP* with minor stylistic changes.

B89 "Over the Sea of Hesitation." *New Yorker* 48 (November 11): 40-43.

B90 "A Man." *New Yorker* 48 (December 30): 26-27.

1973

B91 "The Inauguration." *Harper's* 246 (January): 86-87.

B92 Unsigned "Comment" piece titled "A Made Up Story." *New Yorker* 48 (February 10): 27-28. Rpt. as "The Young Visitirs" [sic] in *GP*.

B93 "The Teachings of Don B.: A Yankee Way of Knowledge." *New York Times Magazine*, February 11, pp. 14-15, 66-67. Rpt. in *GP* with one minor stylistic change.

B94 "The Angry Young Man." *Fiction* 2 (no.2): 7. Rpt. in *GP* with a major rearrangement of paragraphs, minor stylistic changes, additions, and elisions.

B95 "What To Do Next." *New Yorker* 49 (March 24): 35-37. Rpt. in *A* with one minor addition and the elision of the fourth paragraph on p. 35 and the long parenthesis on p. 36 (serial version).

B96 "Our Work and Why We Do It." *New Yorker* 49 (May 5): 39-41. Rpt. in *A* with the change of "Oxford Book of American Sin" to "Oxford Book of American Grub."

B97 "Some of Us Had Been Threatening Our Friend Colby." *New Yorker* 49 (May 26): 39-40. Rpt. in *A*.

B98 "The Educational Experience." *Harper's* 246 (June): 62-65. Rpt. in *A* without collages.

B99 "At the End of the Mechanical Age." *Atlantic* 231 (June): 52-55. Rpt. in *A*.

B100 "That Cosmopolitan Girl." *New Yorker* 49 (July 16): 26-27, signed "Lily McNeil." Rpt. in *GP*.

B101 "You Are Cordially Invited." *New Yorker* 49 (July 23): 33-34. Rpt. in *A*.

B102 "The Discovery." *New Yorker* 49 (August 20): 26-27. Rpt. in *A*.

B103 "A Dream." *New Yorker* 49 (September 3): 25, signed "Lily McNeil." Rpt. in *GP* as "An Hesitation on the Banks of the Delaware" minus the first sentence and with one typographical error corrected ("a head a home" to "a head at home").

B104 "One Hundred Ten West 61st Street." *New Yorker* 49 (September 24): 33-34. Rpt. in *A*, with the addition of a new final paragraph.

B105 "The Wound." *New Yorker* 49 (October 15): 36-37. Rpt. in *A* with the change of "Lady of Perpetual Anguish" to "Lady of the Several Sorrows."

B106 "The Royal Treatment." *New York Times*, November 3, p. 29, signed "Lily McNeil." Rpt. in *GP* with minor stylistic changes.

B107 "And Then." *Harper's* 247 (December): 87-89. Rpt. in *A* with change of "ruin of my father" to "ruin of my anaconda."

B108 Untitled, unsigned "Comment" piece introduced as "a letter from a friend." *New Yorker* 49 (December 24): 29-30. Rpt. in *GP* as "The Palace" with minor stylistic changes.

B109 "Nothing: A Preliminary Account." *New Yorker* 49 (December 31): 26-27. Rpt. in *GP* with one minor elision.

B110 Untitled, unsigned "Comment" piece, bottom of column 2 and top of column 3. *New Yorker* 49 (December 31): 17.

1974

B111 "The Photographs." *New Yorker* 49 (January 28): 32-33. Rpt. in *GP*.

B112 "Letters to the Editore." *New Yorker* 50 (February 25): 34-35. Rpt. in *GP* with the change of "Paula Marf" to "Paula Marx."

B113 "The Bed." *Viva* 1 (March): 68-70.

B114 "You Are as Brave as Vincent Van Gogh." *New Yorker* 50 (March 18): 34. Rpt. in *A*.

B115 "The Reference." *Playboy* 21 (April): 163, 186-187. Rpt. in *A* with one minor elision.

B116 Untitled, unsigned "Comment" piece. *New Yorker* 50 (April 1): 27. Rpt. in *GP* as "Heliotrope," with minor stylistic changes.

B117 "Mr. Foolfarm's Journal." *Village Voice* 19 (May 16): 1, 54. Rpt. in *GP* with minor stylistic changes and one elision.

B118 "Bunny Image, Loss Of: The Case of Bitsy S." First appearance in *GP*.

B119 "The School." *New Yorker* 50 (June 17): 28. Rpt. in *A*.

B120 "The New Member." *New Yorker* 50 (July 15): 28-30. Rpt. in *A*.

B121 "The Agreement." *New Yorker* 50 (October 14): 44-45. Rpt. in *A*.

B122 "I Bought a Little City." *New Yorker* 50 (November 11): 42-44. Rpt. in *A*.

B123 Unsigned, untitled "Comment" piece. *New Yorker* 50 (November 11): 37.

1975

B124 Untitled, insigned "Comment" piece. *New Yorker* 51 (January 19): 21.

B125 "Rebecca." *New Yorker* 51 (February 24): 44-45. Rpt. in *A*.

B126 "Manual for Sons." *New Yorker* 51 (May 12): 40-50. Rpt. in *DF* with two sections placed in a different order and with minor stylistic changes and additions.

B127 "The Great Hug." *Atlantic* 235 (June): 44-45. Rpt. in *A*.

B128 "The Sergeant." *Fiction* 3 (no. 2-3): 24-25. Rpt. in *A* with the change of "I said: Father!" to "I said: Andromache!"

B129 Unsigned, untitled "Comment" piece. *New Yorker* 51 (June 23): 29-30.

B130 Unsigned, untitled "Comment" piece. *New Yorker* 51 (August 11): 19.

B131 Unsigned, untitled "Comment" piece. *New Yorker* 51 (September 29): 27.

B132 Unsigned, untitled "Comment" piece. *New Yorker* 51 (October 20): 31.

1976

B133 "The Dassaud Prize." *New Yorker* 51 (January 12): 26-29.

B134 "Monumental Folly" (with illustrations by Edward Sorel). *Atlantic* 237 (February): 33-40.

B135 "The Short Story Contest." *New York Times Magazine*, February 1, p. 79. Includes two paragraphs of a story, "Manfred," to be completed by contestants.

B136 "Cornell." Joseph Cornell Exhibition Catalogue, Leo Castelli Gallery, New York City [February-March]. Reprinted in *Ontario Review* no. 5 (Fall-Winter), p. 50

B137 "Manfred" (with Karen Shaw). *New York Times Magazine*, April 18, p. 87. Completion of item B135.

B138 "The Great Debate." *New Yorker* 52 (May 3): 34-35.

B139 Unsigned, untitled "Comment" piece. *New Yorker* 52 (June 14): 25-26.

B140 "The Captured Woman." *New Yorker* 52 (June 28): 22-25. Rpt. in *A*.

B141 Unsigned, untitled "Comment" piece. *New Yorker* 52 (July 12): 25-26.

B142 Unsigned, untitled "Comment" piece. *New Yorker* 52 (October 11): 31.

B143 "Belief." University of Houston *Forum* 13 (Winter): 47-49.

C

ESSAYS

C1 "A Note on Elia Kazan." University of Houston *Forum* 1 (September 1956). 19-22.

C2 "Reiner, David," and "Pages from the Annual Report." University of Houston *Forum* 3 (March 1959): 13-18. Unsigned.

C3 "Culture, Etc." *Texas Observer* 51 (March 25, 1960): 7.

C4 "Mr. Hunt's Wooly Utopia." Review of *Alpaca* by H.L. Hunt. *Reporter* 22 (April 14, 1960): 44-46.

C5 "Introduction." *Architectural Graphics.* Catalogue for an exhibition at the Contemporary Arts Museum, Houston, Texas, April 8-29, 1960.

C6 *The Emerging Figure.* Contemporary Arts Museum Catalogue, May-June, 1961. Text reprinted in University of Houston *Forum* 3 (Summer 1961): 23-24.

C7 "The Case of the Vanishing Product." *Harper's* 223 (October 1961): 30-32.

C8 *Ways and Means.* Catalogue for an exhibition at the Contemporary Arts Museum, Houston, October-November 1961.

C9 *Contemporary Arts Museum,* Houston, 1961. An unsigned pamphlet.

C10 "Elaine de Kooning Paints a Picture." Unsigned broadside with photograph and text, ca. June 1962.

C11 *Contemporary Arts Museum Annual Report* 1961-62. Unsigned.

C12 "After Joyce." *Location* 1 (Summer 1964): 13-16.

C13 "The Tired Terror of Graham Greene." Review of *The Comedians* by Graham Greene. *Holiday* 39 (April 1966): 146, 148-149.

C14 "The Elegance Is Under Control." Review of *The Triumph* by John Kenneth Galbraith. *New York Times Book Review*, April 21, 1968, pp. 4-5.

C15 *she*. Preface to an exhibition catalogue of women in art. Cordier & Ekstrom Gallery, New York, December 3, 1970—January 16, 1971. Unpaged.

C16 Untitled commentary on "Paraguay." *Writer's Choice*, edited by Rust Hills (New York: David McKay, 1974), pp. 25-26.

C17 "Robert Morris." *Robert Morris* [an exhibition catalog]. New York: Washburn Gallery, pp. 3-4. February 10 - March 6, 1976.

C18 "A Symposium on Fiction" (with William H. Gass, Grace Paley, and Walker Percy). *Shenandoah* 27 (Winter 1976): 3-31.

D.

DRAMATIC ADAPTION OF A WORK

D1 *Snow White.* A Rehearsed Reading of an In-Progress Work.
The American Place Theatre, New York, New York, Thursday, June 10, 1976, 2:00 PM. Wynn Handman, Director; Julia Miles, Associate Director. Program note: "This Rehearsed Reading of Mr. Barthelme's play is designed to give him an opportunity to participate in rehearsals, see his play with an audience and hopefully use this experience to further the development of the play and of himself as a playwright."

E.

INTERVIEWS WITH DONALD BARTHELME

E1   Baker, John F. "PW Interviews Donald Barthelme," *Publishers Weekly* 206 (November 11, 1974): 6-7.

Barthelme discusses his Houston background, his move to New York and first stories, his association with *The New Yorker* and editor Roger Angell, his appreciation of William H. Gass, Grace Paley, Walker Percy, and John Barth, the National Book Awards, *Guilty Pleasures*, collage stories, Saul Steinberg, work habits, and teaching.

E2   Cross, Leslie. "Down in the Village With Donald Barthelme," *Milwaukee Journal*, February 4, 1973, p. 4, Editorial Section.

At the Cedar Tavern, Barthelme comments on life in Greenwich Village, his Houston years, *Location*, *Fiction*, his teaching, and his apartment.

E3   Klinkowitz, Jerome. "Donald Barthelme," *The New Fiction/Interviews With Innovative American Writers*, edited by Joe David Bellamy (Urbana: University of Illinois Press, 1974), pp. 45-54.

Barthelme describes his youth in Houston, his father and architecture, work on *Forum* and *Location*, his association with *The New Yorker*, how some of his stories are parts of a failed novel, the death of the novel because of a decline in the quality of readership, Kurt Vonnegut's idea of spatial form, Kenneth Koch as a novelist, collage as a principle of art and culture, jazz, influences, and Texas.

E4   Schickel, Richard. "Freaked Out on Barhtelme," *New York Times Magazine*, August 16, 1970, pp. 14-15, 42.

Barthelme's fear of boredom is cited, along with his comments on collage, reading habits, and problems in sustaining a novel.

F.

SOUND RECORDINGS OF DONALD BARTHELME

F1 *New Sounds in American Fiction,* prepared by Gordon Lish, 1969.

Cummings 51612. Addison Wesley Publishing Co. Barthelme reads and discusses his story, "The Piano Player."

F2 *Donald Barthelme I, II, III, and IV.* Pacifica Tape Library, 1976, BC 2720.01-04.

Barthelme reads from *The Dead Father,* discusses his early writings and influences, cinematic techniques in writing, and his attempt to reach a realm of meaning which can't quite be said, as in rendering an emotion by bypassing it. Tape 2: he talks about demands placed upon his readers, surpassing predecessors and himself, the modern American literary scene, found objects in fiction, poorly prepared critics, and also reads from *City Life.* Tape 3: Barthelme discusses parody as fiction or non-fiction, the Lily McNeil pen-name, English as an endangered language, children's books, and how he teaches writing; he reads from *The Slightly Irregular Fire Engine.* Tape 4: Barthelme reads from *Snow White* and *Come Back, Dr. Caligari;* he discusses experiments in narrative form, the use of dreams, the relation of act and history to fiction, and John Barth's re-using of myths.

G.

EARLY WRITINGS IN HOUSTON, TEXAS

1948-1949

G1	"Inertia." Poem which won the Poet Laureate of Texas Award. Not located.
G2	"Integrity Cycle." Story which tied for fourth place in Scholastic Magazine Contest. Not located.
G3	"Rover Boys' Retrogression." *Sequoyha 1948-1949*, pp. 4-7. Parody of *Pilgrim's Progress* with prefatory note on the nature of parody.
G4	"Task." *Sequoyha 1948-1949*, p. 8. Poem.
G5	"Poseur's Progress." *Sequoyha 1948-1949*, p. 9. Poem.
G6	"Love." *Sequoyha 1948-1949*, p. 10. Poem.
G7	"Where Credit Is Due." *Sequoyha 1948-1949*, p. 11. Poem.
G8	"And a Happy New Year." *Sequoyha 1948-1949*, p. 12. Poem.

1950

G9	"Young Author Tells of Southern Decay." *Cougar*, June 16, p. 2. Rev. of *Tiger in the Garden* by Speed Lamkiñ.

G10 "Postwar Germany Pictured by Valtin." *Cougar*, June 23, p. 2. Rev. of *Wintertime* by Jan Valtin.

G11 "Barmaids, Walls and Models Enrich Tale of Frustration." *Cougar*, June 30, p. 2. Rev. of *The Horse's Mouth* by Joyce Cary.

G12 " 'Campus Town' Tells of UT Journalist." *Cougar*, July 8, p. 2. Rev. of *Campus Town*, author not given.

G13 "Princetonian Tells of Literary Minds." *Cougar*, July 14, p. 2. Reviews of *A Long Day's Dying* by Frederick Buechner. No by-line but probably by Barthelme.

G14 "Around and About: Author Hits Cokes for Distinct Gain." *Cougar*, August 18, p. 2. On stealing redeemable coke bottles.

G15 "Around and About: Home Ec Brews Alchemist's Broth." *Cougar*, August 25, p. 2. On a news item in the August 18 *Cougar*, p. 1, "Home Ec to Offer Accessory Design" with announcement of course in alchemy. Column is a playlet, set in the Alchemy lab. First appearance in Barthelme's work of a member of the Pitkin family.

G16 "Around and About: Pitkin Attends Cureall Ball." *Cougar*, September 22, p. 2. On Congressman Ripley J. Unthank's Cureall Ball (a paraody of Hadacol), covered by Scoop Pitkin.

G17 "Around and About: Scribe Turns to Culture, Wincing." *Cougar*, September 29, p. 3. Will write about drama throughout the coming year [as Amusements Editor].

G18 "Around and About: Poll Projects Bleak Future." *Cougar*, October 6, p. 3. Polling Sabatini Pitkin and Rathbone Pitkin on career choices. Soon everyone will be teaching instead of creating art.

G19 "Around and About: On Radio and Rainwater." *Cougar*, October 13, p. 2. On problem of reading poetry on KUHF-FM, the campus radio station, and a response to Clyde Rainwater's letter on the same page complaining that Barthelme thinks he is Wolcott Gibbs and asserting that the east is the only place where culture exists.

G20 "Attic Players Make 'Dinner' a Real Treat." *Cougar*, October 20, p. 3. Rev. of a production of *The Man Who Came to Dinner*.

G21 "'Juliet' In Attic Is A Bit of All Right." *Cougar*, November 3, p. 1. Rev. of a production of *There's Always Juliet* by John Van Druten.

G22 "Through the Years with John FitzPitkin." *Cougar*, November 10, p. 2. History of the Pitkin family.

G23 "On TV and JATP." *Cougar*, November 17, p. 2. Opposing commercials trying to sell television sets and touting the Jazz at the Philharmonic appearance in Houston.

G24 "Life, Times of F.S. Fitzgerald Sparkle in 'The Disenchanted.'" *Cougar*, December 1, p. 2. Rev. of *The Disenchanted* by Budd Schulberg.

G25 "Scribe Describes Rise and Fall of Pitkinetics." *Cougar*, December 1, p. 2. Report on L. Ron Pitkin's "Your Mind: Hell or Haven?" Parody of L. Ron Hubbard's Dianetics.

G26 "'Caesar and Cleopatra' Rehearsal Leaves Much To Be Desired." *Cougar*, December 1, p. 3. Rev. of dress rehearsal of the Shaw play.

G27 "German Writer Visits Campus." *Cougar*, December 7, p. 1. Lieselotte Greger, who worked for *Stars and Stripes*.

G28 "Scarred Scribe Lauds Drama Department." *Cougar*, December 7, p. 2. Defense of his negative review of *Ceasar and Cleopatra*.

1951

G29 "'Trio' Less than 'Quartet' in More Ways Than One, Says Reviewer." *Cougar*, January 5, p. 2. Rev. of *Trio* by W. Somerset Maugham.

G30 "The Shooting of Dan McGroovy." *Cougar*, January 5, p. 2. A retelling, in the style of Damon Runyon, with McGroovy a Dixieland piano player forced to play society music to support Lou.

G31 "On Flair & Apathy." *Cougar*, January 12, p. 2. Photograph of Barthelme. On the collapse of *Flair* and on the dearth of letters to the editor for the *Cougar*.

G32 "Attic Scores with 'Angel Street.'" *Cougar*, January 12, p. 4. Rev. of the Patrick Hamilton play.

G33 "Rattle That Saber, Stoke That Pipe." *Cougar*, January 19, p. 2. Ironic lament that KUHF is not broadcasting Confederate propaganda.

G34 "Muckraker Probes Big Cream Deficit." *Cougar*, January 31, p. 2. Disappearance of cream from the cafeteria. Declares total war on television, having been denied admission to a local channel's party.

G35 "UT Smears UH In 'Texan' Story." *Cougar*, February 9, p. 2. Photograph. Response to Ronnie Dugger's editorial slap at UH as a party school; predicts "a bright future in journalism" for Dugger because he has "a typewriter and no ethics . . . ."

G36 "Attic Successful with Barrie Comedy." Cougar, February 9, p. 4. Rev. of *What Every Woman Knows* by James M. Barrie.

G37 "Savage Whiskers in the Old Corral." *Cougar*, February 16, p. 2. History of fashions in hair and hairlessness. Probably occasioned by the "Bearded Wonder Contest" for the annual Fiesta at the University of Houston.

G38 "On Burnt Jello, Clams, and Poetry." *Cougar*, March 2, p. 2. Poets are becoming more and more inward and should not expect to be read or understood. Socially conscious poets have the advantage of comprehensible content.

G39 "No Thanks, Bill, We Can't Use You." *Cougar*, March 9, p. 2. On the feud between the *Cougar* and the drama department, denying Bill Roberts' assertions in the Houston press.

G40 "Editor's Note" to "Student Gigs Cougar; Cougar Gigs Student" by Henri Gadbois. *Cougar,* March 16, p. 2. Unsigned.

G41 "Rich Roasts Old Friends." *Cougar,* March 16, p. 2. Photograph. On dropping George Rich's column "Call Board" on the grounds that the *Cougar* was giving too much space to drama.

G42 "Attic Presents Play of Small Value." *Cougar,* March 16, p. 5. Rev. of production of *The Young and Fair* by Richard Nash.

G43 "Committee Probes Cougar; More Rich." *Cougar,* March 22, p. 2. Expects no result from the committee appointed by the student assembly. Further attack on George Rich and his associates.

G44 "Editor's Note" to "Gadbois, Groggy but Game, Again Writes to Cougar—Ineptly" by Henri Gadbois. *Cougar,* March 22, p. 2. Correcting grammar and usage. Unsigned.

G45 "Editor's Note" to "Cougar Threatened with Law Suit" by Junne Sims. *Cougar,* March 30, p. 1. Letter demands an apology for a statement [in Bardley's column] in the March 22 *Cougar.* Editor's note: "Anyone for tennis?" Unsigned.

G46 "Editor's Note" to "Gadbois, Our Inept Correspondent, Writes Again; Still Murders Language in His Inimitable Way." *Cougar,* March 30, p. 2. Unsigned

G47 "He'd Ban Magazine If He Had Library." *Cougar,* April 6, p. 2. Attacks *New American Mercury* editor William Bradford Huie for offering to attack any college which bans the magazine from its library.

G48 "Our Choice: Go Broke or Starve." *Cougar,* April 13, p. 2. Editorial complaining about cafeteria food prices.

G49 "A Modest Proposal for Short Tables." *Cougar,* April 13, p. 6. Responding to a complaint that new tables in the cafeteria are not long enough for sororities, proposes sororities small enough for the tables.

G50 "'Liliom' Charming in Cullen Theatre." *Cougar*, April 20, p. 4. Rev. of production of the Frederic Molnar play.

G51 "The Sky Hasn't Fallen." *Cougar*, May 4, p. 2. Editorial condemning the so-called solution to the dormitory residents' strike over cafeteria prices.

G52 "Probe Where Probe Is Due, Sans Spotlight." *Cougar*, May 4, p. 2. Editorial criticizing investigation of Communist influence on movies because of headline-seeking attention to actors (instead of to more potentially responsible writers and directors).

G53 "The Joe Engberg Story." *Cougar*, May 4, p. 2. Wrote "On the Con" for the *Cougar;* has disappeared.

G54 "Paging Sam Goldwyn." *Cougar*, May 11, p. 2. Parody of movie fad of "bold" movie themes.

G55 "The Old Order Is Clobbered." *Cougar*, June 8, p. 2. On being deposed from editorship.

G56 "Our Own Air War," *Cougar*, June 15, p. 2. On American difficulty in turning things off, especially radios. Suggests a course in the process.

G57 "K-K-K-K-K-K-Katie." *Cougar*, June 29, p. 2. Slash at Kate Smith Show as shredding traditional expectations of Americans for their stars.

G58 "Grimm Revisited." *Cougar*, July 13, p. 2. Jane, a witch, fails in her attempt to steal a child and is drummed out of witches' union.

G59 Note to Len Stewart, "Bardley Gigged by Smith Fan." *Cougar*, July 13, p. 2.

G60 "Familiar Quotations." *Cougar*, July 20, p. 2. English major's interruption to question word usage upset whole *Cougar* schedule.

G61 "Majestic Gets Robert Ryan As a Good Man Gone Wrong." *Post*, July 20, sec. 1, p. 14. Rev. of *Best of the Badmen.*

G62 "'Inheritance' a Danse Macabre With Some Villainous Partners." *Post*, July 26, sec. 2, p. 2. Rev. of *The Inheritance.*

G63 "The Kaye Killings." *Cougar,* July 27, p. 3. Attack on Houston *Chronicle* for thinking that "bebop" caused a gang fight. Suggests Sammy Kaye music as cause of mass murders.

G64 "Nostalgic 'On Moonlight Bay' At Majestic With Doris Day." *Post,* July 27, sec. 1, July 27, sec. 1, p. 17. Rev. of *On Moonlight Bay.*

G65 "'Half Angel' a Pleasant Fantasy at Metropolitan." *Post,* July 27, sec. 1, p. 17. Rev. of *Half Angel* with Loretta Young.

G66 "'Garden' Gets a Grim Visitor in 'Death Takes a Holiday.'" *Post,* August 1, sec. 3, p. 4. Rev. of Garden Theatre production of Alberto Easella play.

G67 "'Teresa' Poignant Film Drama With Excellent New Actress." *Post,* August 2, sec. 1, p. 10. Rev. of *Teresa* with Pier Angeli.

G68 "'Francis Goes to the Races' Gay Sweepstakes at Loew's." *Post,* August 9, sec. 2, p. 11.

G69 "Goodbye, Plato." *Cougar,* August 10, p. 5. "Philosophy" was an excuse for goofing off in old cafeteria. The new one is too clean to think in.

G70 "Agile Lady In Enticing Role at Met." *Post,* August 10, sec. 1, p. 17. Rev. of *The Prince Who Was a Thief* with Piper Laurie. Story credited to Theodore Dreiser.

G71 "Greer Garson a Shady Lady in Doubtful Game at Loew's." *Post,* August 16,, sec. 3, p. 2. Rev. of *The Law and the Lady.*

G72 "John Ireland Carries Word to Custer at Metropolitan." *Post,* August 17, sec. 2, p. 9. Rev. of *Little Big Horn.*

G73 "Mr. Disney's 'Wonderland' With Charm at Majestic." *Post,* August 17, sec. 2, p. 9. Rev. of *Alice in Wonderland.*

G74 "Torture!" *Cougar,* August 24, p. 2. Running out of material, he may steal from Milton, partly because he suspects that *Paradise Lost* is "one huge joke." May introduce Lucifer Pitkin.

G75 "Abbott and Costello in Mountain Turkey Trot at the Majestic." *Post,* August 24, sec. 1, p. 16. Rev. of *Comin' Round the Mountain.*

G76 "Singer Jane Powell at Loew's As Beautiful Texan in Paris." *Post,* August 30, sec. 2, p. 2. Rev. of *Rich, Young and Pretty.*

G77 "Jeanne Crain As Sorority Girl at Met." *Post,* August 31, sec. 2, p. 11. Rev. of *Take Care of My Little Girl.*

G78 "Canny Spencer Tracy Breaks An Air-Tight Case at Loew's." *Post,* September 6, sec. 1, p. 14. Rev. of *The People Against O'Hara.*

G79 "Majestic Gets Dean Martin and Jerry Lewis Impersonating Big Men on the Campus." *Post,* September 7, sec. 2, p. 6. Rev. of *That's My Boy.*

G80 "'Hunchback of Notre Dame' With Charles Laughton This Week." *Post,* September 9, sec. 5, p. 2. Also previews *Peking Express; Jim Thorpe, All American; Cattle Drive.* Photograph of Barthelme.

G81 "'Kiss and Tell' With Charm at the Garden Theatre." *Post,* September 12, sec. 2, p. 4. Rev. of production of F. Hugh Herbert play.

G82 "'Cattle Drive' a Departure in Western Films at Loew's." *Post,* September 13, sec. 2, p. 5.

G83 "Morcopi." *Cougar,* September 14, p. 2. Title is condensation of "More copy." Advice to new freshmen: go home.

G84 "Burt Lancaster in 'Jim Thorpe—All American' Displays Gridiron Statesmanship at Met." *Post,* September 14, sec. 3, p. 3.

G85 "Grisly Thriller Among Week's Films; Plenty of Music for Relief." *Post,* September 16, sec. 5, p. 2. Previews of *Five* and *Pickup.* Photograph of Barthelme.

G86 "Sin." *Cougar,* September 21, p. 2. Photograph. On styles of writing produced by various typewriters. Mentions bands coming to Houston, notably Stan Kenton's.

G87 "Fast Tour of Show Business With Betty Grable at Majestic." *Post*, September 21, sec. 2, p. 6. Rev. of *Meet Me After the Show*.

G88 "Marriage for Cash Treated Brilliantly in 'Pickup.'" *Post*, September 23, sec. 5, p. 2.

G88a "'People Will Talk' at Majestic Bright Slice of Adult Comedy," *Post*, September 28, sec. 2, p. 14. With Cary Grant, Jeanne Crain.

G89 "Stage Business." *Post*, September 30, sec. 5, p. 4. The first of Barthelme's Sunday columns on local stage events, replacing Pandora, "Backstage Patter."

G90 "Jeff Chandler as Ring Killer In 'Iron Man' at Loew's." *Post*, October 4, sec. 1, p. 15.

G91 "Van Heflin Loses to the Law In 'The Prowler' at Majestic." *Post*, October 5, sec. 2, p. 7.

G92 "Stage Business." *Post*, October 7, sec. 5, p. 4.

G93 "Shamrock Gets Rather Mystic Ballet from Trio," *Post*, October 10, sec. 3, p. 9. Naldi, Mary Kaye, and Vanya.

G94 "Paul Douglas Cops Pennant At Loew's." *Post*, October 11, sec. 1, p. 15. Rev. of *Angels in the Outfield*.

G95 "Step Right Up." *Cougar*, October 12, p. 2. Reviews *Gentry*, a pretentious new Time, Inc. journal.

G96 "Singing Newsman Bing Crosby In Pursuit of Jane Wyman." *Post*, October 12, sec. 3, p. 11. Rev. of *Here Comes the Groom*.

G97 "Howard Hill on Stage at Met With Full Quiver and 'Tembo.'" *Post*, October 12, sec. 3, p. 11. Hill an archer; appeared in, produced film.

G98 "UH Farce Engaging Brawl." *Post*, October 16, sec. 3, p. 3. Rev. of production of *See How They Run* by Philip King.

G99 "Gable Turns Explorer For 'Across the Wide Missouri,'" *Post*, October 18, sec. 1, p. 10.

G100 "Vera-Ellen Gets Her Man In Musical Whirl at Met." *Post*, October 19, sec. 1, p. 18. Rev. of *Happy Go Lovely*.

G101 "Stage Business." *Post*, October 21, sec. 5, p. 3.

G102 "Space Visitor Panics Earth In Science Fiction Film" *Post*, October 24, sec. 2, p. 7. Rev. of *The Day the Earth Stood Still*.

G103 "Dennis Morgan Runs Musical Footrace In 'Painting the Clouds With Sunshine.'" *Post*, October 26, sec. 2, p. 9.

G104 "Stage Business." *Post*, October 28, sec. 5, p. 3.

G105 "'Rhubarb' Good Fun at Met." *Post*, October 30, sec. 1, p. 8. Rev. of film with Ray Milland.

G106 "'Granz' 'Jazz at the Philharmonic' Brings Uneven Music Hall Evening." *Post*, October 31, sec. 2, p. 10.

G107 "Murder." *Cougar*, November 2, p. 2. On the tradition of not smiling in the *Cougar* office being killed by a sign advising the staff to smile.

G108 "'The Desert Fox' Pictures Last Days of Erwin Rommel." *Post*, November 2, sec. 1, p. 16.

G110 "Stage Business." *Post*, November 4, sec. 5, p. 2.

G111 "Taut 'Giaconda Smile' on View at University." *Post*, November 6, sec. 3, p. 7. Rev. of production of play adapted from the Aldous Huxley story.

G112 "Sam's Song." *Cougar*, November 9, p. 2. Announces his plan for a dictionary of cliches. Photograph.

G113 "James Cagney As City Editor At Majestic." *Post*, November 9, sec. 2, p. 6. Rev. of *Come Fill the Cup*.

G114 "Stage Business." *Post*, November 11, sec. 4, p. 2.

G115 "Elwood P. Dowd and Friend Pay a Visit to Music Hall." *Post*, November 13, sec. 1, p. 15. Rev. of *Harvey* with an all-Negro company.

G116 "Dirty Edna." *Cougar*, November 16, p. 2. Begun and ended by Barrister Pitkin, his attorney, including Bardley's statement about the progress of his research for the "Chicks Are No Damn Good Society." Is cliche-gathering. Photograph.

G117 "Kirk Douglas at Majestic In Ugly 'Detective Story.'" *Post*, November 16, sec. 2, p. 9.

G118 "Stage Business." *Post*, November 18, sec. 5, p. 2.

G119 "Puppetry With Skill at UH." *Post*, November 20, sec. 1, p. 15. Rev. performance of Salzburg Marionette Theatre.

G120 "Telegraft." *Cougar*, November 21, p. 2. Series of telegrams between Bardley and the *Cougar* editor about what to print instead of Bardley's column. Last is sent from Reading Gaol.

G121 "Expert Latin Dance Work at Music Hall." *Post*, November 21, sec. 1, p. 6. Rev. of performance of Ana Maria's Spanish Ballet.

G122 "Van Johnson Unearths A Prodigy at Loew's." *Post*, November 22, sec. 1, p. 17. Rev. of *Too Young to Kiss* with June Allyson.

G123 "Delman Gets Brisk Comedy About Thugs." *Post*, November 22, sec. 1, p. 17. Rev. of *Behave Yourself*.

G124 "Cochran Takes Armor Into Latter-Day Indian Country." *Post*, November 23, sec. 2, p. 7. Rev. of *The Tanks Are Coming* with Steve Cochran.

G125 "Stage Business." *Post*, November 25, sec. 5, p. 2.

G126 "Spike Jones and Company In Strenuous Concert." *Post*, November 28, sec. 2, p. 9.

G127 "Bulletin." *Cougar*, November 30, p. 2. Special dispatch about Bardley's charge that the British are plotting "to emasculate American taste, intelligence and morale" by exporting the works of John Milton.

G128 "Mitzi Gaynor Glitters at Met; Majestic Gets Star Shower." *Post*, November 30, sec. 3, p. 9. Rev. of *Golden Girl;* at Majestic, *Starlight*.

G129 "Stage Business." *Post*, December 2, sec. 5, p. 3.

G130 "Fry Comedy With Verve At University of Houston." *Post*, December 4, sec. 2, p. 7. Rev. of production of *A Phoenix Too Frequent* by Christopher Fry.

G131 "Macdonald Carey Recovers Outlaw Gold at Loew's." *Post,* December 6, sec. 4, p. 2. Rev. of *Cave of Outlaws.*

G132 "Jailbreak." *Cougar,* December 7, p. 2. Series of parody excerpts of various magazine reports of Bardley's escape from Reading Gaol.

G133 "Claudette Colbert Endures Marital Difficulties at Met." *Post,* December 7, sec. 3, p. 9. Rev. of *Let's Make It Legal.*

G134 "Stewart Granger an Art-Lover With Sticky Fingers at Met." *Post,* December 13, sec. 2, p. 11. Rev. of *The Light Touch.*

G135 "Majestic Gets Apocalypse; Pitfalls of Cinema at Met." *Post,* December 14, sec. 3, p. 8. Rev. of *When Worlds Collide.* Second film, *The Strip,* reviewed by G.C. [George Christian].

G136 "Stage Business." *Post,* December 16, sec. 5, p. 3.

G137 "Symphony Performs With Distinction In Tenth Subscription Concert." *Post,* December 19, sec. 4, p. 9.

G138 "Dane Clark as Head Gunman In Above-Average Western." *Post,* December 20, sec. 4, p. 11. Rev. of *Fort Defiance.*

G139 "Gene Tierney Attempts an Adoption In 'Close to My Heart' at Metropolitan." *Post,* December 21, sec. 4, p. 9.

G140 "Ballet Russe In Glowing Performance." *Post,* December 28, sec. 3, p. 7.

G141 "Stage Business." *Post,* December 30, sec. 6, p. 3.

1952

G142 "Robert Taylor Nursemaids a Wagon Train." *Post,* January 1, sec. 4, p. 3. Rev. of *Westward the Women.*

G143 "Gary Cooper Thins the Ranks of the Seminole Indians." *Post,* January 2, sec. 4, p. 3. Rev. of *Distant Drums.*

G144 "Stage Business." *Post,* January 6, sec. 6, p. 3.

G145 "Visit With Ice Royalty: Sonja Henie in Town." *Post,* January 8, sec. 3, p. 5.

G146 "'Drunkard' a Comic Uproar At the Melodrama Theatre." *Post,* January 10, sec. 2, p. 9.

G147 "Goodbye to All That." *Cougar,* January 11, p. 2. Pseudo-British, clipped account of his escape and return. Discovered a beautiful new language in *Paradise Lost.*

G148 "'The Racket' Rough, Bloody." *Post,* January 11, sec. 4, p. 2. With Robert Mitchum, Robert Ryan.

G149 "Stage Business." *Post,* January 13, sec. 6, p. 2.

G150 "Bette Davis Chill Menace In 'Another Man's Poison." *Post,* January 18, sec. 4, p. 4.

G151 "Bob Hope In Spy Intrigue At Majestic." *Post,* January 18, sec. 4, p. 4. Rev. of *My Favorite Spy.*

G152 "Stage Business." *Post,* January 20, sec. 5, p. 2.

G153 "Youth Symphony Performs With Credit at Music Hall." *Post,* January 22, sec. 1, p. 4.

G154 "Brisk Humor at Majestic in 'Room for One More.'" *Post,* January 25, sec. 4, p. 2. With Cary Grant.

G155 "Richard Basehart at Met. As Infantryman in Korea." *Post,* January 25, sec. 4, p. 2. Rev. of *Fixed Bayonets.*

G156 "Stage Business." *Post,* January 27, sec. 5, p. 3.

G157 "Organist Claire Coci Makes Eloquent Concert Appearance." *Post,* January 30, sec. 4, p. 3.

G158 "Greetings." *Cougar,* February 1, p. 2. Mentions law suit against him for $50,000. Various Pitkins recur. Freshmen go home. Photograph.

G159 "Stage Business." *Post,* February 7, sec. 3, p. 10.

G160 "Singing Cadets Excellent In San Jacinto Concert." *Post,* February 8, sec. 3, p. 8. Rev. of Texas A & M Glee Club concert.

G161 "Stage Business." *Post,* February 10, sec. 6, p. 3.

G162 "Evening of Impressive Performances At Concert of Chamber Music Guild." *Post,* February 13, sec. 3, p. 4.

G163 "Pablo and Me." *Cougar,* February 15, p. 2. On demise of his Picasso reproduction.

G164 "'I Want You' a Film Drama of the Higher Order at Met." *Post,* February 15, sec. 3, p. 9.

G165 "Stage Business." *Post,* February 17, sec. 5, p. 3.

G166 "Billy Eckstein Wows Packed City Auditorium in Concert." *Post,* February 20, sec. 2, p. 7.

G167 "Stage Business." *Post,* February 21, sec. 3, p. 9.

G168 "'Phone Call From a Stranger' Rewarding Exhibit at Met." *Post,* February 22, sec. 1, p. 9. With Bette Davis.

G169 "Stage Business." *Post,* February 24, sec. 5, p. 2.

G170 "Expert Version of 'Escape' On View in Attic Theatre." *Post,* February 26, sec. 3, p. 5. Rev. of production of John Galsworthy play.

G171 "'Cello-Piano Duo Warmly Received." *Post,* February 28, sec. 3, p. 8. Rev. of performance by Joanna and Nikolai Graudan.

G172 "Stage Business." *Post,* March 2, sec. 6, p. 3.

G173 "Stage Business." *Post,* March 9, sec. 6, p. 3.

G174 "Stage Business." *Post,* March 11, sec. 3, p. 7.

G175 "Ray Milland Battles Sioux Nation at Met." *Post,* March 14, sec. 3, p. 5. Rev. of *Bugles in the Afternoon.*

G176 "Stage Business." *Post,* March 16, sec. 6, p. 2.

G177 "Stage Business." *Post,* March 23, sec. 6, p. 3. Dateline in newpaper is, mistakenly, March 16.

G178 "NY Times Critic Delivers Thoughtful UH Address." *Post,* March 27, sec. 4, p. 2. Music critic Olin Downes.

G179 "Visitant." *Cougar,* March 28, p. 2. A flamingo may be the reincarnated "archy" of Don Marquis creation. Sample of poem. Bardley has been too busy meditating for several weeks to write.

G180 "Kettles Go to the Fair." *Post,* March 28, sec. 3, p. 11. Rev. of *Ma and Pa Kettle at the Fair.*

G181 "Kirkland Play Gets Able UH Performance." *Post,* April 1, sec. 2. p. 5. Rev. of performance of *Suds in Your Eye* by George Kirkland.

G182 "Boys' Choir Scores at Music Hall." *Post,* April 2, sec. 3, p. 7. The Singing Boys of Norway.

G183 "Princeton Chorus Delivers Lively San Jacinto Concert." *Post,* April 4, sec. 3, p. 11.

G184 "Stage Business." *Post,* April 6, sec. 6, p. 1.

G185 "Youth Group in Spirited Concert." *Post,* April 8, sec. 3, p. 6. Houston Youth Symphony.

G186 "Spring Song." *Cougar,* April 10, p. 2. Story of Henry Rue and Caprice Pitkin; she leaves him after taking a new dramatic role: Nora. Photograph.

G187 "Fairy Tale In Film at Met." *Post,* April 11, sec. 3, p. 12. Rev. of *Jack and the Beanstalk.*

G188 "Stage Business." *Post,* April 13, sec. 6, p. 4.

G189 "Gene Austin a Hit at Shamrock." *Post,* April 16, sec. 3, p. 7. Also on bill: Eileen and Carver, acrobatic dancers.

G190 "'Love Rides the Rails' A Hit at Melodrama." *Post,* April 18, sec. 3, p. 9.

G191 "Stage Business." *Post,* April 20, sec. 6, p. 2.

G191a "Star-Studded Sermon at River Oaks." *Post,* April 20, sec. 6, p. 3. Rev. of *It's a Big Country.*

G192 "Sister Act at Shamrock." *Post,* April 30, sec. 3, p. 5. The five DeMarco sisters.

G193 "Epitaph." *Cougar,* May 2, p. 2. Capture of last poet and burning of last poem. New rules for "½oetry" and "½oets." [*Sic*] Science triumphs, but "the strain on birds, flowers and sunsets" is so great that they are all used up.

G194 "'Macao' an Exotic Affair." *Post,* May 2, sec. 3, p. 9. With Robert Mitchum and Jane Russell.

G195 "Shrunken Clocks for Small Hours," *Harvest,* 17 (1952), 18. Poem. See also Barthelme's response in "Our Contributors," p. 84.

G196 "'Death of a Salesman' Powerful Film Drama." *Post,* May 4, sec. 6, p. 3.

G197 "Stage Business." *Post,* May 4, sec. 6, p. 3.

G198 "Albino Torres in Satisfying Piano Recital." *Post,* May 6, sec. 3, p. 5.

G199 "Steinbeck Drama Given Expert UH Production." *Post,* May 7, sec. 4, p. 3. Rev. of production of *Of Mice and Men.*

G200 "Outstanding Jazz Concert in Auditorium." *Post,* May 9, sec. 3, p. 9. Louis Armstrong and his group.

G201 "'Home With Bonny Jean': Houston Singer Makes 'Brigadoon' a Career." *Post,* May 11, sec. 6, p. 2. Singer is John Taliaferro.

G202 With George Christian. "Met Caravan Brings Some Lively Stars." *Post,* May 13, sec. 3, p. 5. Among others, Leonard Warren, Patrice Munsel, and Robert Merrill.

G203 "Myrna Loy At Met; Gunplay at Majestic." *Post,* May 16, sec. 4, p. 3. Rev. of *Red Mountain* with Alan Ladd and Lizbeth Scott and *Belles on Their Toes* with Loy.

G204 "Stage Business." *Post,* May 18, sec. 6, p. 2.

G205 "University Lyric Festival Gets a Lively Start." *Post,* May 21, sec. 2, p. 7.

G206 "Battle for Timber at Met." *Post,* May 23, sec. 3, p. 11. Rev. of *The Big Trees.*

G207 "Stage Business." *Post,* May 25, sec. 6, p. 2.

G208 "'Maru Maru' A Rousing Action Film." *Post,* May 30, sec. 2, p. 7. With Errol Flynn.

G209 "Stage Business." *Post,* June 1, sec. 8, p. 3.

G210 "Peter Lawford in Lively Comedy at Met." *Post,* June 6, sec. 3, p. 11. Rev. of *Just This Once.* With Janet Leigh.

G211 "Artie Shaw Writes of His Inner Self." *Post,* June 8, sec. 7, p. 6. Rev. of *The Trouble With Cinderella.*

G212 "Stage Business." *Post,* June 8, sec. 8, p. 2.

G213 "Pop Records." *Post,* June 8, sec. 8, p. 3. Features Peggy Lee's version of "Lover" and the Billy May Orchestra.

G214 "Singer Tito Guizar a Hit in Emerald Room." *Post,* June 11, sec. 3, p. 5. With George and Vivian Proctor, acrobatic dancers.

G215 "Firefighters Stage Civil War at Met." *Post,* June 13, sec. 3, p. 5. Rev. of *Red Skies of Montana.*

G216 "Stage Business." *Post,* June 15, sec. 8, p. 2.

G217 "Ronald Reagan Pitching Tight Game at Met." *Post,* June 20, sec. 3, p. 5. Rev. of *The Winning Team* with Doris Day.

G218 "Stage Business." *Post,* June 22, sec. 8, p. 2. Photograph of Barthelme.

G219 "Film Stars in Town For Theatre Opening." *Post,* June 24, sec. 2, p. 7. Tim Holt, Coleen Gray for opening of King Drive-In Theatre.

G220 "Comic Operas Get Expert Performance." *Post,* June 25, sec. 3, p. 5. Rev. of Houston Music Theatre productions of Menotti's *The Old Maid and the Thief* and Offenbach's *R.S.V.P.*

G221 "Randolph Scott at Majestic; Music at Met." *Post,* June 27, sec. 3, p. 5. Rev. of *Carson City* and *About Face.*

G222 "Stage Business." *Post,* June 29, sec. 8, p. 2.

G223 "Pop Records." *Post,* June 29, sec. 8, p. 2. Features "Free Forms" with Ralph Burns and Lee Konitz; Merv Griffin's "Mama's Gone, Goodbye"; a Perry Como-Eddie Fisher duet; Charlie Spivak Orchestra.

G224 "High-Spirited 'Kangaroo' at the Metropolitan." *Post,* July 4, sec. 1, p. 7. With Peter Lawford and Maureen O'Hara.

G225 "Stage Business." *Post,* July 6, sec. 8, p. 3. Photograph.

G226 "Singer Nick Lucas a Hit in the Shamrock Room." *Post,* July 9, sec. 2, p. 6. With dancer Nita Bieber and the Nat Brandywynne Orchestra.

G227 "Paul Douglas, Robert Ryan in Violent Amours at Met." *Post,* July 11, sec. 3, p. 5. Rev. of *Clash by Night.*

G228 "Stage Business." *Post,* July 13, sec. 8, p.3.

G229 "Blood-Letting in Haiti: Tense Drama at Majestic." *Post,* July 18, sec. 3, p. 5. Rev. of *Lydia Bailey.*

G230 "Stage Business." *Post,* July 20, sec. 8, p. 3. Photograph.

G231 "English Comic a Hit in Shamrock Room." *Post,* July 23, sec. 2, p. 7. Comedian Rex Ramer; singer Louise Martell.

G232 "Ranchers, Farmers Clash Again in Majestic Film." *Post,* July 25, sec. 2, p. 7. Rev. of *Untamed Frontier* with Shelley Winters.

G233 "Dance Team Scores in Rice Room." *Post,* July 25, sec. 2, p. 7. Carlos and Linda, comic dancers.

G234 "Stage Business." *Post,* July 27, sec. 8, p. 3. Photograph.

G235 "New Academy Theatre Makes Informal Debut." *Post,* July 30, sec. 2, p. 7. New movie house.

G236 "Lance Against Lance at Ashby: Loew's Gets a Brave Spectacle." *Post,* August 1, sec. 2, p. 7. Rev. of *Ivanhoe.*

G237 "Stage Business." *Post,* August 3, sec. 8, p. 3. Photograph.

G238 "Emerald Room Gets a Lively Twin Bill." *Post,* August 6, sec. 3, p. 5. Singer-dancer-pianist Johnny Bachemin; singer Constance Moore.

G239 "Majestic Gets Impressive Biography of Will Rogers." *Post,* August 8, sec. 2, p. 7. Rev. of *The Story of Will Rogers.*

G240 "Stage Business." *Post,* August 10, sec. 8, p. 3. Photograph.

G241 "Maestro Harry James Offers Lively Revue." *Post,* August 13, sec. 2, p. 7.

G242 "Great Stone Face Back in New Comedy at Met." *Post*, August 15, sec. 4, p. 7. Rev. of *Dreamboat* with Clifton Webb.

G243 "No Peaks, No Valleys and Only One Color in Thomas Sterling's Novel." *Post*, August 17, sec. 7, p. 5. Rev. of *Strangers are Afraid*.

G244 "Stage Business." *Post*, August 17, sec. 8, p. 3. Photograph.

G245 "UH Farce Pleasant, Lively." *Post*, August 19, sec. 3, p. 5. Rev. of production of *Gammer Gurton's Needle*.

G246 "Moving Film Version of 'Carrie.'" *Post*, August 22, sec. 2, p. 7. Rev. of *Carrie*, based on Theodore Dreiser's *Sister Carrie*.

G247 "Grenadine's Progeny Not up to Original." *Post*, August 24, sec. 7, p. 5. Rev. of *Grenadine's Spawn* by Robert Ruark.

G248 "Stage Business." *Post*, August 24, sec. 8, p. 3. Photograph.

G249 "Nina Vance Confirmed as Alley 'Manager.'" *Post*, August 26, sec. 3, p. 5.

G250 "Dashing Gregory Peck Visits Alaska at Met." *Post*, August 29, sec. 2, p. 7. Rev. of *The World in His Arms*, based on the Rex Beach novel.

G251 "Stage Business." *Post*, August, 31, sec. 7, p. 3. Includes a mock version of *The Old Man and the Sea* as done by Mike Todd.

G252 "Delegates From Broadway Success at Shamrock." *Post*, September 3, sec. 2, p. 7. "What's New," a company of six.

G253 "Talented Vocalists Take Debut Bows at Rice." *Post*, September 5, sec. 2, p. 7. Betty Jane Watson and Jerry Austen appearing at the Rice Hotel Empire Room.

G254 "Stage Business." *Post*, September 7, sec. 8, p. 3. Photograph.

G255 "Youth Group Opens New Season." *Post*, September 23, sec. 2, p. 7. Houston Youth Symphony.

G256 "Junketing Film Producer Discusses Animals, Stars." *Post*, September 24, sec. 3, p. 11. Jerry Wald, touting *The Lusty Men*.

G257 "Homecoming." *Cougar*, September 26, p. 2. Editor asked him to return to give the *Cougar* some needed nastiness.

G258 "'Fearless Fagan' Pleasant Bit of Comedy at Loew's." *Post*, September 26, sec. 3, p. 11. Fagan is a lion.

G259 "Burt Lancaster in Violent, Comic Story of Piracy." *Post*, September 26, sec. 3, p. 11. Rev. of *The Crimson Pirate*.

G260 "Stage Business." *Post*, September 28, sec. 7, p. 3. Photograph.

G261 "Lively Kean Sisters Score at Shamrock." *Post*, October 1, sec. 3, p. 9. Comedy act.

G262 "Homecoming." *Cougar*, October 3, p. 2. Introduces an 82-year-old Young Republican and announces his own intention to run for the highest office in the land—at the top of the Empire State Building.

G263 "Brisk Comeday at Majestic; Intrigue Simmers at Loew's." *Post*, October 3, sec. 2, p. 7. Rev. of *Monkey Business* and of *The Devil Makes Three*.

G264 "Garay a Hit in Empire Room Debut." *Post*, October 3, sec. 2, p. 7. Joaquin Garay, singer.

G265 "Stage Business." *Post*, October 5, sec. 8, p. 3. Photograph.

G266 "Novel." *Cougar*, October 10, p. 2. Chapter one of his decadent Southern novel, *Amanda Feverish*.

G267 "Strong Version of 'Big Sky' Now on View at Majestic." *Post*, October 10, sec. 3, p. 11. Rev. of film version of A.B. Guthrie novel.

G268 "Stage Business." *Post*, October 12, sec. 8, p. 3. Photograph.

G269 "'Arsenic and Old Lace' With Spirit at University." *Post*, October 14, sec. 3, p. 5. Rev. of production of Joseph Kesselring play.

G270   "Panic." *Cougar,* October 17, p. 2. Chapter two of *Amanda Feverish.*

G271   "'Quiet Man' Strong Drama; Audie Murphy at Majestic." *Post,* October 17, sec. 2, p. 9. Rev. of *The Quiet Man* with John Wayne and of *Duel at Silver Creek.*

G272   "Stage Business." *Post,* October 19, sec. 8, p. 3. Photograph. Science fiction version of Goldilocks.

G273   "'Solid' Evening with Wayne King and Friends." *Post,* October 21, sec. 1, p. 6. Rev. of band and show.

G274   "Visitation." *Cougar,* October 24, p. 2. Chapter three of *Amanda Feverish.*

G275   "Mario Lanza in Comedy at Loew's." *Post,* October 24, sec. 2, p. 9. Rev. of *Because You're Mine.*

G276   "Another Huckster Handout." *Post,* October 26, sec. 7, p. 7. Rev. of *The Quick Brown Fox* by Lawrence Schoonover.

G277   "Stage Business." *Post,* October 26, sec. 8, p. 3. Photograph.

G278   "Good Hoofer at Shamrock." *Post,* October 29, sec. 2, p. 7. Paddy Wing, Chinese tap dancer; Day Dreamers quartet.

G278a "Finale." *Cougar,* October 31, p. 2. End of *Amanda Feverish,* "which may be the only four-chapter novel in the entire world."

G279   "Loew's Gets Musical; Majestic a War Film." *Post,* October 31, sec. 3, p. 5. Rev. of *Everything I Have is Yours; One Minute to Zero* reviewed by George Christian.

G280   "Baritone Eric Thorsen a Hit." *Post,* October 31, sec. 3, p. 5. At the Empire Room, Rice Hotel.

G281   "Stage Business." *Post,* November 2, sec. 8, p. 3.

G282   "Hemingway on Film, With Gregory Peck." *Post,* November 5, sec. 3, p. 7. Rev. of *The Snows of Kilimanjaro.*

G283   "Gary Cooper Cashiered in New Majestic Film." *Post*, November 7, sec. 3, p. 9. Rev. of *Springfield Rifle*.

G284   "Stage Business." *Post*, November 9, sec. 8, p. 2.

G285   "Orchestra with Spirit." *Post*, November 11, sec. 2, p. 7. Houston Youth Symphony.

G286   "Bret Harte Story Makes Strong Film." *Post*, November 14, sec. 3, p. 7. Rev. of *The Outcasts of Poker Flat*.

G287   "'Oklahoma!' in Empire Room." *Post*, November 14, sec. 3, p. 7. Three-person version.

G288   "Young Viennese Pianist in Expert Performance." *Post*, November 20, sec. 3, p. 8. Paul Badura-Skoda.

G289   "Espionage at Leow's, Majestic." *Post*, November 21, sec. 3, p. 7. Rev. of *The Thief* with Ray Milland and of *Operation Secret*.

G290   "Stage Business." *Post*, November 23, sec. 8, p. 3. Photograph.

G291   "Lady with Real Wit a Hit at Shamrock." *Post*, November 26, sec. 2, p. 5. Mary McCarty, comedienne; Eddie Peabody, banjo king.

G292   "Actress, Back from Korea, Wants to Play Europe Next." *Post*, November 27, sec. 3, p. 6. Michele Condre, Houston actress.

G293   "Met Gets Fresh Comedy in 'The Happy Time.'" *Post*, November 28, sec. 4, p. 3. Based on the play by Samuel Taylor.

G294   "Jim Bowie Story at Majestic." *Post*, November 28, sec. 4, p. 3. Rev. of *The Iron Mistress*.

G295   "Hollywood: Two Views Behind the Movie Scene." *Post*, November 30, sec. 7. p. 5. Rev. of *Picture, A Story about Hollywood* by Lillian Ross; *The Magic Lantern* by Robert Carson rev. by Shirley K. Sullivan.

G296   "Stage Business." *Post*, November 30, sec. 8, p. 3. Photograph.

G297 "Sparkling 'Varsity Varieties' Debuts in University's Cullen Auditorium." *Post,* December 5, sec. 4, p. 3. Sponsored by University of Houston journalism organizations.

G298 "Stage Business." *Post,* December 7, sec. 8, p. 4. Photograph.

G299 "Ted Lewis and Company A Hit at Shamrock." *Post,* December 10, sec. 4, p. 3.

G300 "Frontier Gunman Lauded in New Majestic Offering." *Post,* December 12, sec. 4, p. 3. Rev. of *The Lawless Breed,* about John Wesley Hardin.

G301 "Stage Business." *Post,* December 14, sec. 7, p. 4. Photograph.

G302 "John Crosby Takes on Role of Gadfly." *Post,* December 14, sec. 7, p. 5. Rev. of *Out of the Blue* by John Crosby.

G303 "University Offers Solid Staging of Kingsley Plan." *Post,* December 16, sec. 3, p. 9. Rev. of production of *Detective Story* by Sidney Kingsley.

G304 "Damon Runyon Story of Majestic: 'Bloodhounds' Bright Comedy." *Post,* December 19, sec. 4, p. 3. Rev. of *Bloodhounds of Broadway.*

G305 "Stage Business." *Post,* December 21, sec. 7, p. 4.

G306 "Musicala Hit at Alley." *Post,* December 28, sec. 6, p. 1. Rev. of *Burlesque.*

G307 "Stage Business." *Post,* December 28, sec. 6, p. 2. Photograph.

1953

G308 "Overflow Crowd Hears a Brilliant Concert." *Post,* January 7, sec. 2, p. 7. E. Power Biggs at First Presbyterian Church.

G309 "Abbott, Costello and Co. Do It Again at Majestic." *Post,* January 9, sec. 3, p. 5. Rev. of *Abbott and Costello Meet Captain Kidd.*

G310   "Stage Business." *Post,* January 11, sec. 7, p. 3. Photograph.

G311   "Combat Clips Lend Force to 'Flat Top' at Met." *Post,* January 16, sec. 3, p. 5.

G312   "Stage Business." *Post,* January 18, sec. 7, p. 2. Photograph.

G313   "Warm Reception for Diva in the Shamrock Room." *Post,* January 21, sec. 3, p. 9. April Stevens, with Bernie George, impressionist, and Margaret Brown, ballet-tap dancer.

G314   "'Cousin Rachel' in Deadly Visit at the Met." *Post,* January 23, sec. 2, p. 7. Rev. of *My Cousin Rachel.*

G315   "Alan Ladd Thwarts Plot, Captures a Bride at Met." *Post,* January 23, sec. 2, p. 7. Rev. of *Thunder in the East.*

G316   "Colorful Riverboat Story in 'Mississippi Gambler.'" *Post,* January 30, sec. 3, p. 5. With Tyrone Power.

G317   "Stage Business." *Post,* February 1, sec. 7, p. 2. Photograph.

G318   "Alley Honors Members at First Award Dinner." *Post,* February 3, sec. 2, p. 7.

G319   "Golden West Cowboys Mount Emerald Room Bandstand." *Post,* February 4, sec. 2, p. 7. Pee Wee King and his orchestra during week of Fat Stock Show.

G320   "Scott Does it Again in New Film at Met." *Post,* February 6, sec. 3, p. 9. Rev. of the *Man Behind the Gun* with Randolph Scott.

G321   "Stage Business." *Post,* February 8, sec. 7, p. 4. Photograph.

G322   "Stage Business." *Post,* February 15, sec. 7, p. 4. Photograph.

G323   "Harrison, Palmer Sparkle in 'The Four Poster.'" *Post,* February 18, sec. 2, p. 7.

G324   "Goldwyn Does it Again." *Post,* February 20, sec. 1, p. 9. Rev. of *Han Christen Andersen.*

G325 "Stage Business." *Post,* February 22, sec. 7, p. 3. Photograph.

[February 1953 to January 1955, Military Service]

1955

G326 "Drama in Alley's Arena Respectable Sarte." *Post,* January 18, sec. 4, p. 6. Rev. of production of *The Flies* by Jean-Paul Sartre.

G327 "Mr. Coward: The March of Time." *Post,* January 20, sec. 4, p. 5. Rev. of production of *Design for Living* by Noel Coward.

G328 "Range War Opens at Majestic." *Post,* January 21, sec. 2, p. 7. Rev. of *The Violent Men.*

G329 "Stage Business," *Post,* January 23, sec. 5, p. 7. Photograph. Dateline on page is January 30.

G330 "Calleia May Prove Good Luce Piece." *Post,* January 23, sec. 5, pp. 7, 9. Joseph Calleia in *All My Sons.*

G331 "Stage Business." *Post,* January 30, sec. 5, p. 11.

G332 "Stage Business." *Post,* February 6, sec. 5, p. 9. Photograph.

G333 "Notes on Planning from Famed Architect." *Post,* February 8, sec. 1, p. 9. The architect is Richard Neutra.

G334 "Interesting Concert from Youth Players." *Post,* February 8, sec. 2, p. 7. Houston Youth Symphony.

G335 "Halls of Montezuma Revisited in 'Cry.'" *Post,* February 11, sec. 3, p. 11. Rev. of *Battle Cry.*

G336 "Stage Business." *Post,* February 13, sec. 5, p. 9. Photograph.

G337 "Concert of Dimensions from French Organist." *Post,* February 16, sec. 4, p. 7. Jeanne Demessieux at the First Presbyterian Church.

G338 "Stage Business: Angels to Dallas; Barnes for 'Dial.'" *Post,* February 20, sec. 5, p. 9.

G339 "The Face of Innocence in a Substantial Film Drama." *Post,* February 22, sec. 4, p. 7. Rev. of *The Little Kidnappers.*

G340 "Stage Business." *Post,* February 27, sec. 5, p. 9. Photograph.

G341 "Tiny Diva Warms Shamrock." *Post,* March 4, sec. 1, p. 11. Maureen Cannon, with Bill Finch, dancer and baton twirler.

G342 "Stage Business." *Post,* March 6, sec. 5, p. 9. photograph.

G343 "Faltering 'Peer Gynt' on University Stage." *Post,* March 10, sec. 3, p. 8. Rev. of University of Houston production of Ibsen play.

G344 "Pianists in Brilliant Recital." *Post,* March 11, sec. 2, p. 9. Arthur Gold and Robert Fizdale, dual pianists.

G345 "Sioux Rout Cavalry in Met Film." *Post,* March 11, sec. 2, p. 9. Rev. of *Chief Crazy Horse.*

G346 "Stage Business." *Post,* March 13, sec. 5, p. 11. Photograph.

G347 "University Dance Band in Sterling Concert." *Post,* March 17, sec. 1, p. 16. At the University of Houston Spring Arts Festival.

G348 "The Syndicate Probed in 'Confidential.'" *Post,* March 18, sec. 2, p. 7. Rev. of *New York Confidential.*

G349 "Stage Business." *Post,* March 20, sec. 5, p. 9. Photograph. Photograph, not identified by name in "The Guidepost," sec. 1, p. 1.

G350 "Brilliant Pianist in Tuesday Club Event." *Post,* March 22, sec. 4, p. 7. Seymour Lipkin performance.

G351 "Outer Space Revisited: 'Conquest' At Met." *Post,* March 25, sec. 4, p. 9. Rev. of *Conquest of Space.*

G352 "Singing Duo Opens in Rice Empire Room." *Post,* March 25, sec. 4, p. 9. Mary Martha Briney and Bob Carter.

G353 "Stage Business." *Post,* March 27, sec. 5, p. 11. Photograph.

G354 "ANTA'S 'Album' Nice, But no World-Beater." *Post,* March 29, sec. 4, p. 5. Features Lena Horne, Ruth Draper, and Victor Borge as best.

G355 "Chanson-Chanter Scores a Hit in Shamrock Room." *Post,* April 1, sec. 2, p. 9. Jenny Collins.

G356 "Pretty Bella Darvi in New Met Film." *Post,* April 1, sec. 2, p. 9. Rev. of *The Racers* with Kirk Douglas.

G357 "Stage Business." *Post,* April 3, sec. 5, p. 11. Photograph.

G358 "Empire Room Gets Circus in Miniature." *Post,* April 8, sec. 4, p. 8.

G359 "Stage Business." *Post,* April 10, sec. 5, p. 10. Photograph.

G360 "William Inge Discusses Plays and Writing." *Post,* April 12, sec. 1, p. 8. Inge staying at the Shamrock on way to do screenplay of *Bus Stop.*

G361 "Spanish Dancing with Gusto." *Post,* April 15, sec. 2, p. 8. "Spanish Fantasy" troupe.

G362 "Stage Business." *Post,* April 17, sec. 5, p. 7. Photograph.

G363 "Met Tenor in Concert of Brio." *Post,* April 19, sec. 2, p. 8. Jan Peerce at Music Hall.

G361 "Brilliant Film from Elia Kazan." *Post,* April 21, sec. 1, pp. 8-9. Rev. of *East of Eden.*

G365 "Crime Film on Display at Met." *Post,* April 22, sec. 4, p. 11. Rev. of *Gangbusters.*

G366 "Stage Business." *Post,* April 24, sec. 5, p. 9. Photograph.

G367 "Novelties Enliven Youth Group Fete." *Post,* April 27, sec. 1, p. 8. Houston Youth Symphony in Spring Music Festival.

G368 "Heartbalm for the Indian, from an Old H'wood Recipe." *Post*, April 28, sec. 6, p. 8. Rev. of *White Feather*.

G369 "Bright Piano Recital; Saunders' Season Told." *Post*, April 29, sec. 4, p. 9. Pianist is Rudolf Firkusny.

G370 "Music Hall Performance of 'Mutiny' is Absorbing Drama." *Post*, April 30, sec. 1, p. 10. Rev. of performance of *The Caine Mutiny* with William Bendix and James Bumgarner.

G371 "Stage Business." *Post*, May 1, sec. 5, p. 9. Photograph.

G372 "Shep Fields, Dancers on New Rice Bill." *Post*, May 6, sec. 4, p. 7.

G373 "Stage Business." *Post*, May 8, sec. 5, p. 8.

G374 With Christian, George. "Met's Robinson, Warren, Talk about the Opera." *Post*, May 10, sec. 2, p. 7. Francis Robinson is Tour Director.

G375 "Nimble-Fingered Mr. Maxwell A Hit in Shamrock Room." *Post*, May 13, sec. 2, p. 7. Robert Maxwell, harpist, with Betty Madigan, singer.

G376 "Stage Business." *Post*, May 15, sec. 5, p. 7.

G377 "Respectable 'Macbeth' on Cullen Auditorium Stage." *Post*, May 19, sec. 4, p. 9. Rev. of University of Houston production.

G378 "Acrobats in Empire Room Opening." *Post*, May 20, sec. 2, p. 7. Maggie and Bernie Harris.

G379 "Mr. Astaire Steps Out at Majestic." *Post*, May 20, sec. 2, p. 7. Rev. of *Daddy Long Legs*.

G380 "Stage Business." *Post*, May 22, sec. 5, p. 13. Photograph.

G381 "Into the Air with SACman J. Stewart." *Post*, May 27, sec. 2, p. 10. Rev. of *Strategic Air Command*.

G382 "John Wayne Goes to the Bottom at Met." *Post*, May 27, sec. 2, p. 10. Rev. of *The Sea Chase*.

G383 "Stage Business." *Post*, May 29, sec. 5, p. 7. Photograph.

G384   "Stage Business." *Post,* June 5, sec. 5, p. 4. Photograph.

G385   "'Davy' Parker Pauses Briefly at Airport." *Post,* June 7, sec. 4, p. 7. Fess Parker, who played Davy Crockett in Disney films and on television.

G386   "Comic Mime Brightens Shamrock Supper Club." *Post,* June 10, sec. 2, p. 8. Will Jordan, with Sinclair and Spaulding, dancers.

G387   "No Ears, No 'Ole's [sic] for 'Magnificent Matador.'" *Post,* June 10, sec. 2, p. 8. Rev. of *The Magnificent Matador.*

G388   "Stage Business." *Post,* June 12, sec. 5, p. 7. Photograph. Unidentified photograph in "The Guidepost," sec. 1, p. 1.

G389   "James Brings Variety to Music Hall Stage." *Post,* June 16, sec. 4, p. 9. Harry James band and road show.

G390   "Joyce Cary." *Post,* June 19, sec. 5, p. 4. Review of *Not Honour More.*

G391   "Stage Business." *Post,* June 19, sec. 5, p. 9.

G392   "Stage Business." *Post,* June 26, sec. 5, p. 11.

G393   "Guests Help 'Androcles' in Cullen Auditorium." *Post,* June 30, sec. 3, p. 5. Rev. of University of Houston production of *Androcles and the Lion* by George Bernard Shaw.

G394   "Excellent 'Mr. Roberts' on View at Majestic." *Post,* July 1, sec. 3, p. 2.

G395   "Stage Business." *Post,* July 3, sec. 5, p. 7. Photograph.

G396   "Lewis, Clark Junket at Metropolitan." *Post,* July 8, sec. 4, p. 8. Rev. of *The Far Horizons* with Charlton Heston and Fred MacMurray.

G397   "Stage Business." *Post,* July 10, sec. 5, p. 8.

G398   "Met's 'Man' in Classic Tradition." *Post,* July 15, sec. 1, p. 10. Rev. of *The Man From Laramie* with Jimmy Stewart.

G399 "Stage Business." *Post,* July 17, sec. 5, p. 11. Photograph.

G400 "Undulating Lady Sparks 'Itch' at Majestic." *Post,* July 22, sec. 1, p. 10. Rev. of *The Seven Year Itch* with Marilyn Monroe.

G401 "Stage Business." *Post,* July 24, sec. 5, p. 11. Photograph.

G402 "Ambiguous 'Pete Kelly' on View at Metropolitan." *Post,* July 29, sec. 2, p. 8. Rev. of *Pete Kelly's Blues* with Jack Webb.

G403 "Age and Stage of Harrigan and Hart." *Post,* July 31, sec. 5, p. 4. Rev. of *The Merry Partners* by E.J. Kahn, Jr. Late nineteenth century stage figures.

G404 "Stage Business." *Post,* July 31, sec. 5, p. 9. Photograph.

G405 "Stage Business: Ex-Playhouse Men on B'way; Albus Touring." *Post Now,* August 7, p. 33. Photograph. *Now* is a tabloid-sized supplement to the Sunday edition of the *Post.*

G406 "'Lady and the Tramp' Wows the Younger Set." *Post,* August 12, sec. 2, p. 10. Rev. of Disney movie.

G407 "Stage Business: Morgan Heads Committee; Norton to Tulsa." *Post Now,* August 14, p. 32. Photograph.

G408 "'Damask Cheek' Offered on University Stage." *Post,* August 18, sec. 4, p. 9. Rev. of University of Houston production of *The Damask Cheek* by John Van Druten.

G409 "Peggy Ryan and Friend Open in Shamrock Room." *Post,* August 19, sec. 2, p. 8. Peggy Ryan and Ray McDonald, song and dance act; singer Ethel Rider.

G410 "Stage Business." *Post Now,* August 21, p. 32. Photograph.

G411 "Grable, North in Slow College Film at the Met." *Post,* August 26, sec. 1, p. 13. Rev. of *How to be Very, Very Popular.*

G412 "Stage Business: 'Tea' Mixup; Piaf Coming." *Post Now,* August 28, p. 29. Photograph.

G413   "Therapy in Cheesecloth, or How to Banish Worry and Spur Album Sales." *Post,* September 1, sec. 2, p. 13. On the trend in "music that *does* something for you."

G414   "Top-Flight Show Debuts at the Shamrock-Hilton." *Post,* September 2, sec. 2, p. 8. Cardini, magician, and Mary Meade, singer and impressionist.

G415   "Stage Business: Revue Set; MacAgy En Route." *Post Now,* September 4, p. 26. Dr. Jermayne MacAgy, first professional director of the Contemporary Arts Museum.

G416   "Word from California: The Impala is Jumping and the Cotton is High." *Post,* September 7, sec. 3, p. 11. On publicity material from Hollywood studios.

G417   "Opera Chief Here with Plans for New Season." *Post,* September 9, sec. 4, p. 7. Walter Herbert.

G418   "Hank Fort in Empire Room." *Post,* September 9, sec. 4, p. 7.

G419   "Stage Business: Influx from Cripple Creek." *Post Now,* September 11, p. 33. Photograph.

G420   "Scott Fitzgerald and the Screen: Where is the Flickering Light?" *Post,* September 13, sec. 1, p. 10. Photograph. Discussion of *The Last Time I Saw Paris* [adapted from "Babylon Revisited"] and Mercedes McCambridge's television version of *Tender is the Night.*

G421   "Gunsmoke on the Ginza with Bob Ryan, Friends." *Post,* September 16, sec. 1, p. 11. Rev. of *House of Bamboo.*

G422   "Stage Business: Standing Ovation for Stoky." *Post Now,* September 18, p. 31. Photograph.

G423   "Pleasant Maugham Story at the River Oaks." *Post,* September 21, sec. 4, p. 9. Rev. of *The Beachcomber.*

G424   "Jennifer Jones, William Holden in Hong Kong." *Post,* September 23, sec. 4, p. 7. Rev. of *Love is a Many Splendored Thing.*

G425   "Stage Business: Danilova Dancing in Manila." *Post Now,* September 25, p. 34. Photograph.

G426 "Spirited Season Opener." *Post*, September 27, sec. 4, p. 7. Houston Youth Symphony.

G427 "Stage Business: 'Sky' Stars Repeat in Dallas." *Post Now*, October 2, p. 34. Photograph.

1956

G428 "'What Has Happened to Cougar?' Remarks Old Guard." *Cougar*, January 20, p. 2. The *Cougar* is now mature and dull. Lists former eccentric staff members. Reprise of themes from his Bardley columns.

G429 "Cameras in the Classroom." *Forum* (Houston), 1, no. 1 (September 1956), 5-8. Unsigned; identified as Barthelme's by Farris Block.

G430 *Graphic Arts & Your Future*. Houston, n.d. Undated and unsigned pamphlet, probably c. 1957, describing the program in Graphic Arts offered by the Department of Journalism and Graphic Arts of the University of Houston. According to S. Wayne Taylor, written and designed by Barthelme.

SECONDARY SOURCES—HOUSTON YEARS

G431 Group photograph of Freshman One-A, including Barthelme; identified as "Literary" reporter on "The Eagle." *The 1946 Aquin* (St. Thomas High School, Houston, Texas), v. 2. Unpaged.

G432 Group photograph of Sophomores Two-A, including Barthelme; listed under "Features" on reproduced masthead of "The Eagle" and in group photograph, with tape on the right side of his face, of the staff. *Aquin*, v. 3 (1947).

G433 Group photograph of Juniors/Eleven-A, including Barthelme without glasses. Listed as one of three writers under "Features" in "The Eagle" masthead; not in group photograph.

G434 "Sheppard, Preston, Eastridge Ranked Among Top Poets." *Lamar Lancer* (Lamar High School, Houston, Texas), 9, no. 13 (April 13, 1949), 1. The award of Texas Poet Laureate "went to Don Barthelme for his poem 'Inertia' on the subject of world cooperation."

G435 "Fascinating Futures Seen For Seniors." *Lamar Lancer*, 9, no. 16 (May 25, 1949), 5. Class prophecy; Barthelme wins a year's supply of laundry soap for a jingle.

G436 Photograph of Barthelme in Senior Class listing, p. 19; photograph in the *Sequoyha* section, p. [78]; photograph, "Don Barthelme, winner of the Poet Laureate Award Contest of Texas," p. [152]. *Orenda* (Lamar High School), 1949.

G437 "Varsity Varieties Appoints Mercer," *Cougar* (University of Houston), 28, no. 3 (September 29, 1950), 1. Barthelme, a sophomore in journalism, is named to script committee with Joe Maranto, George Rich, and Tommy Mercer.

G438 "New Era: Bardley In, Maranto Out." *Cougar*, 29, no. 34 (April 20, 1951), 1. Joe Maranto resigns to take a job with the Houston *Post*; Barthelme, "a 20-year-old sophomore journalism major, is the youngest student in the COUGAR'S history to hold the position of editor."

G429 "Cougar Staff," *Houstonian* (University of Houston yearbook), 17 (1951), 346. Listed as "Managing Editor." No photograph.

G440 Chapman, John. "Reporter Spears a Bubble," *Cougar*, 29, no. 42 (June 22, 1951), 2. Even though Norman Mailer was recommended to him by Bardley, Chapman dislikes Mailer's emphasis on sex and obscenity.

G441 Noack, Eddie. "Old Bardley's Never Die," *Cougar*, 30 (February 15, 1952), 2.

G442 Bedell, W. D. "UH Student Writing Is Artful and Mature," Houston *Post*, May 11, 1952, section 6, p. 5. Review of *Harvest 1952*. Although Robert Vigus' "The Broad Sunlit Uplands" won the Dillon Anderson award for poetry, "Don Barthelme of THE POST seems to have written the best poem of all, 'Shrunken Clocks for Small Hours,' a questioning look at two years of 'cigarette sand . . . and coffee spilled in an excess of feeling.' Few have grasped a truth in such small compass.''

G443 Hollis, Bob. "Literary Anthology Lacks Good Writers," *Cougar*, 30, no. 32 (May 16, 1952), 3. Review of *Harvest 1952*. "Don Barthelme wrote a shallow, cynical piece about 'Shrunken Clocks for Small Hours.' Apparently an attempt to be blase and sophisticated, the bit wobbles dangerously and finally collapses for want of anything to support it."

G444 "The Cougar," *Houstonian*, 18 (1952), 192. Listed as a columnist. Photograph.

G445 Bedell, W.D. "A Deeply Disturbing Novel of the South," Houston *Post*, May 25, 1952, sec. 6, p. 5. Review of Charles Mills, *The Alexandrians*. Does not mention Barthelme, but clearly a source for his parody, "Amanda Feverish: A Deeply Disturbing Novel of the South."

G446 Noack, Eddie. "Welcome, Freshmen," *Cougar*, 30, no. 35 (June 13, 1952), 2. " . . Bardley has retired to his mountain retreat at Polk and Dowling . . . " or the *Post* offices.

G447 Christian, George. "Mr. Runyon's Lively Characters Capering On the Screen Again," Houston *Post*, December 14, 1952, sec. 7, p. 4. ". . . Mr. Barthelme . . . is official Damon Runyon scholar here. . . . "

G448 Rich, George. "Stage Business," Houston *Post*, March 22, 1953, sec. 7, p. 3. "Don Barthelme, whose literary footgear this scrivener is attempting to fill, now at Camp Polk, La. drafted. . . . "

G449 Noack, Eddie. "Thanks. . . . " *Cougar*, 31, no. 36 (May 27, 1954), 2. Lists, among friends, George Christian and Barthelme.

G450 Sims, Junne. "Ex-Cougar Chief Recalls Turbulent 'Good Ol' Days," *Cougar*, 33, no. 4 (October 8, 1954), 2. Letter to the editor reminiscing about the days of Christian, Maranto, and Barthelme and calls for more humor in the comtemporary *Cougar*.

G451   Lacy, Ben. "Bitter Bile Gone Forever," *Cougar*, 33, no. 11 (November 24, 1954), 2. Lists Bardley among "Cougar Stars."

G452   Rich, Leslie. "Stage Business: Bob Ross to Hollywood Oct. 17 For 'Rainmaker' Auditions," Houston *Post Now*, October 9, 1955, p. 33. "In case you're wondering about the strange man peering at you from the top of the column, this reporter, for the second time, has the honor of trying to replace the old master, Don Barthelme, as proprietor of this space . . . Don, who is now making life worth living at the UH news bureau, is not an easy man to follow."

G453   "University Magazine To Be Published in September," *Acta Diurna* (University of Houston), 6, no. 44 (August 22, 1956), 2. Announces the beginning of *Forum*.

G454   "Fill Fourth Estate Jobs in All Parts of Country," *Cougar*, Publications Issue, 35, no. 15 (January 25, 1957), 3. "Helen Barthelme, former UH News Service director, is now associated with Betty Jane Mitchell Advertising Agency. Don Barthelme is still with the University's news office, serving as editor of Acta Diurna and the new faculty magazine, Forum."

G455   "About Former Contributors," *Harvest* 22 (1958), 151. "DON BARTHELME is editor of the quarterly published by UH, *The Forum* . . ."

G456   "U.H. Quarterly Wins Honors In Competition," Houston *Chronicle*, July 14, 1959, sec. 1, p. 16. Not seen.

G457   Judge of Cover Design, *Harvest*, 24 (1960), 5.

G458   "Recognition for Harvest Writers and Editors," *Harvest*, 24 (1960), 125. "DON BARTHELME, who was published in the '52 *Harvest* and has served for two years as editor of the UH quarterly, the *Forum*, has had an article recently in the *Reporter*."

G459   "Barthelme Named by Museum," Houston *Post*, March 23, 1961, sec. 7, p. 4. Barthelme "was one of the principal designers of the museum's new diversification program. The program was adopted by the board last fall. It places equal emphasis on all forms of contemporary expression."

G450 "Barthelme Acting Museum Director," Houston *Chronicle*, March 23, 1961, sec. 5, p. 3.

G451 "Barthelme Quits CAA For NY Job," Houston *Post*, September 15, 1962. In the *Post* file; apparently not printed in the microfilmed Final edition.

G462 "Exit Director, Enter Guests," Houston *Chronicle*, Zest Magazine, September 16, 1962, p. 10.

G463 McCorquodale, Ellen. "Texan Goes to New York To Put Art Magazine on Stands," Houston *Chronicle*, October 2, 1963, sec. 7, p. 6.

G464 Houston, Kathleen E. "Sixteen Outstanding American Writers: Houston Writer Places Second in Annual Contest," Houston *Chronicle*, Zest Magazine, April 16, 1967, p. 14. Barthelme receives second prize in the O. Henry awards for "See the Moon."

G465 Martin, Euford. "Money Isn't Everything," Houston *Chronicle*, Zest Magazine, June 4, 1967, p. 25. Review of *Snow White*.

G466 Waldron, Ann. "The Barthelmes, Houston's Own Hardy Boys," Houston *Chronicle*, Zest Magazine, August 30, 1970, p. 30. Discusses the activities of Donald Barthelme and his siblings.

H.

BIBLIOGRAPHIES OF DONALD BARTHELME

H1 Klinkowitz, Jerome. "Donald Barthelme: A Checklist, 1957-1974." *Critique* 16 (no. 3, 1975): 49-58.

H2 ———. *Literary Disruptions/The Making of a Post-Contemporary American Fiction* (Urbana: University of Illinois Press, 1975), pp. 212-217.

H3 McCaffery, Larry. "Donald Barthelme, Robert Coover, William H. Gass: Three Checklists," *Bulletin of Bibliography* 31 (July/September, 1974): 101-106.

I.

ANNOTATED CHECKLIST OF CRITICAL ESSAYS ON DONALD BARTHELME

I1 Aldridge, John W. "Donald Barthelme and the Doggy Life." *The Devil in the Fire: Retrospective Essays on American Literature and Culture* (New York: Harper's Magazine Press, 1972), pp. 261-266. Rpt. from *Atlantic* 222 (July 1968): 89-91.

Barthelme, Heller, and their colleagues "continue to seem notable more for their potential than for their clearly major distinction." Black Humor "Suddenly . . . seemed capable of registering only the histronics of a ritual angst, a merely ornamental, because creatively unearned, absurdity, a sleek couturier note of apocalypse." Of these writers, Barthelme is "the most interesting because he has the talent and intelligence occasionally to overcome its worst defects." Some of his early stories "brilliantly demonstrate the power of sheer creative imagination to make the connection between satire and the social world." Many stories, however, are "victimized by the fallacy of imitative form."

I2 Bocock, Maclin. "'The Indian Uprising' or Donald Barthelme's Strange Object Covered with Fur." *Fiction International* no. 4/5 (1975), pp. 134-146.

The greatest problem for Barthelme's heroes is sexual scorn by their partners, paralleling Barthelme's relationship to the world at large.

I3 Dickstein, Morris. "Fiction Hot and Kool: Dilemmas of the Experimental Writer." *TriQuarterly* no. 33 (Spring 1975), pp. 257-272.

Barthelme's fictions operate as pure artifice, but at the same time display recognizable characters and themes. Yet Barthelme is no mere collector but a writer "who juxtaposes strange forms and fragments in a way that creates new forms and releases new meanings." Thereby he finds new imaginative life in the contemporary wasteland.

I4 Ditsky, John M. "'With Ingenuity and Hard Work, Distracted': The Narrative Style of Donald Barthelme." *Style* 9 (Summer 1975): 388-400.

The heart of Barthelme's fiction is his style, whether pastiche, fantastic linguistic transports, or "aggregation of materials as a hedge against the fact of nothingness."

I5 Doxey, W. S. "Donald Barthelme's 'Views of My Father Weeping': A Modern View of Oedipus." *Notes on Contemporary Literature* 3 (no. 2, 1973): 14-15.

I6 Flowers, Betty. "Barthelme's *Snow White:* The Reader-Patient Relationship." *Critique* 16 (no. 3, 1975): 33-43.

The modern reader, bored with familiar archetypes, demands the colorful and bizarre, which Barthelme supplies in *SW*. His characters are aware of themselves both as mythical and psychological types. Language is used as pure technique and as a trap for the reader.

I7 Gass, William H. "The Leading Edge of the Trash Phenomenon." *Fiction and the Figures of Life* (New York: Knopf, 1970), pp. 97-103. Rpt. from *The New York Review of Books* 10 (April 25, 1968): 5-6.

"Barthelme has managed to place himself at the center of modern consciousness. Nothing surrealistic about him, his dislocations are real, his material quite actual."

I8 Gillen, Francis. "Donald Barthelme's City: A Guide." *Twentieth Century Literature* 18 (January 1972): 37-44.

An important influence on Barthelme is the "full impact of mass media pop culture on the consciousness of the individual who is so bombarded . . . that he can no longer distinguish the self from the surroundings." His stories in *UP* and *CL* explore the "narrow line between the real and the unreal" in city life.

I9   Gilman, Richard. "Fiction: Donald Barthelme." *The Confusion of Realms* (New York: Random House, 1969), pp. 42-50. Rpt. from *The New Republic* 156 (June 3, 1967): 27-29.

Barthelme reflects a new reality with a new literary imagination. *SW* reflects its own existence as artifiact, since reality "no longer sustain the values necessary" for the creation of representational art.

I10   Graff, Gerald. "Babbitt at the Abyss: The Social Context of PostModern American Fiction." *TriQuarterly* no. 33 (Spring 1975), pp. 305-337.

"*SW* is, in many respects, *Babbitt* brought up to date for an age of bourgeois alienation and self-consciousness." Similar elements are the subjects parodied and the reliance upon irony. Barthelme's special theme is "the comic impossibility of heroism in a world paralyzed by self-consciousness," a theme also explored by Saul Bellow.

I11   _____. "The Myth of the PostModernist Breakthrough." *TriQuarterly* no. 26 (Winter 1973), pp. 383-417.

Barthelme's fiction uses the tools of earlier literary periods, especially nihilistic and skeptical premises.

I12   Guerard, Albert J. "Notes on the Rhetoric of Anti-Realistic Fiction." *TriQuarterly* no. 30 (Spring 1974), pp. 3-50.

Barthelme discovers new fictional modes as he presides over the death of the genre. But unlike Beckett, he is a "cheerful historian of collapse."

I13   Harris, Charles B. *Contemporary American Novelists of the Absurd* (New Haven: College and University Press, 1971), pp. 24, 124-127.

SW "denies the possibility of meaning in an absurd world. The form of his novel thus becomes an analogue to the absurd human condition."

I14   Hassan, Ihab. *Contemporary American Literature* (New York: Frederick Ungar, 1973), pp. 56, 64, 82, 84, 171.

Barthelme's fiction is that of "absurdist humor." He "experiments with non-linear narratives and absurdist techniques ... while maintaining his commitment to a world wildly out of joint." He is more interested in human experience than in value judgments.

I15 ──────. *Paracriticisms* (Urbana: University of Illinois Press, 1975), pp. 44, 58, 82-83, 87, 101, 109, 141.

Barthelme, by evading old critical categories, is Post-Modern. His fictions "have conditioned us to desperate burlesque humor," causing us to ignore his hidden visionary qualities and convert him to Camp.

I16 Hendin, Josephine. "Angries: S-M as a Literary Style." *Harper's* 248 (February 1974): 87-93.

Barthelme sees anger "as the only irresistible emotion," an attitude deriving from the tensions of contemporary American urban life. His fictions disdain life; "he aestheticizes even his depressions." Meaninglessness is Barthelme's conceptual and emotional answer to rage. He sees evil, anger, and death at the human center.

I16a Johnson, R. E., Jr. "'Bees Barking in the Night': The End and Beginning of Donald Barthelme's Narrative." *Boundary 2* 5 (Fall 1976): 71-92.

The seemingly confused narrative of Barthelme's work is in fact structured by an "awareness of the intersubjective dimension of language and a constant vision of the problematical nature" of discourse. "The Balloon" and "The Glass Mountain" eschew plot in favor of game playing which creates a presence for the author in these works, but as created by the reader. Thinking fights with grammar.

I17 Kazin, Alfred. *Bright Book of Life: American Novelists and Storytellers from Hemingway to Mailer* (Boston: Atlantic/Little, Brown, 1973), pp. 38, 183, 271-274.

Barthelme's use of the fragments of our system creates a language powerful beyond the people who use it. He has stripped literature down to the absurd, "operating by countermeasures only."

I18 Klinkowitz, Jerome. "Donald Barthelme's SuperFiction." *Critique* 16 (no. 3, 1975): 5-18.

Barthelme's alleged fragments are actually linguistic signals from our culture, showing the true reality of lives we lead. His stories are deft statements about life's idiosyncracies, which draw their substance from the routine matters noted in other departments of *The New Yorker.*

I19 ———. "Innovative Short Fiction: 'Vile and Imaginative Things.'" *Innovative Fiction* (New York: Dell, 1972), pp. xv-xxvii.

Recent innovative fiction initiates man into the new world created by twentieth-century science. Barthelme's own fiction uses the imagination to recover specific experiences for the life of art, which is otherwise seen as impossible by traditional standards. He "revitalizes tired forms by toying with imaginative content," so that the human ego might once more relate to the world.

I20 ———. "Literary Disruptions; Or, What's Become of American Fiction?" *Partisan Review* 40 (no. 3, 1973): 433-444. Revised and expanded in *Surfiction,* edited by Raymond Federman (Chicago: Swallow Press, 1975), pp. 165-179.

In a time when people no longer believe that fiction expresses the truth of their lives, Barthelme reinvents the genre so that it expresses primarily the truth of its own artificial self. He draws attention to the form of language and the arbitrary conventions of our culture.

I21 ———. "Donald Barthelme." *Literary Disruptions/ The Making of a Post-Contemporary American Fiction* (Urbana: University of Illinois Press, 1975), pp. 62-81.

Barthelme, by focusing on nonlinear form and the imaginative play of language, makes himself the model of Kurt Vonnegut's Tralfamadorian novelist, a master of spatial form. His modifications of language remind us how arbitrary language is, and how reality itself is merely the sum of cultural conventions. Barthelme's fiction revitalizes language so that it is equal to our needs, making us less alienated from the contemporary world. His story "Robert Kennedy Saved from Drowning" is an exercise in failed epistemology, while "Views of My Father Weeping" and *SW* are lessons in how to imaginatively perceive the world.

I22 Krupnick, Mark C. "Notes from the Funhouse." *Modern Occasions* 1 (Fall 1970): 108-112.

"The jokes and poses of imagination at the end of its tether have become both the means and the end in the new fiction, but the comedy has already begun to wear thin." Barthelme does artfully portray the junk of contemporary life, but he "has no opposing images of passion or aesthetic bliss to redeem all this *dreck*." His "self-congratulatory narcissism" is becoming an exhausted mode, confirming us in "the triviality of our confusions."

I23   Lingeman, Richard. "Steal My Name and You Got Trash." *New York Times Book Review*, February 3, 1974, p. 39.

A satirical reply to Barthelme's letter of December 23, 1973, p. 17.

I24   Longleigh, Peter L., Jr. "Donald Barthelme's *Snow White*." *Critique* 11 (no. 3, 1969): 30-34.

SW is largely concerned with linguistic and epistemological questions; "Language and knowledge seem the *topoi* . . . of the book."

I25   McCaffery, Larry. "Barthelme's *SW*: The Aesthetics of Trash." *Critique* 16 (no. 3, 1975): 19-32.

SW examines its own condition as it is created, questioning its own ability to communicate. Barthelme manipulates myth for his own comic purposes. The fairy tale proves unsuccessful because contemporary life cannot sustain a hero. His final purpose is to demonstrate the bankruptcy of language and literary tradition.

I26   Moran, Charles. "Barthelme the Trash-Man: The Uses of Junk." *CEA Critic* 36 (May 1974): 32-33.

Barthelme's prose is essentially fun, which teaches one to appreciate the trash as literary collage. It reminds us not to take ficition too seriously.

I27   Oates, Joyce Carol. "Whose Side Are You On?" *New York Times Book Review*, June 4, 1972, p. 63.

Barthelme's devotion to fragments is irresponsible in view of the real need for artistic responsibility, lest life begin to imitate his art.

I28   Olderman, Raymond M. *Beyond the Waste Land: The American Novel in the 1960's* (New Haven: Yale University Press, 1972), pp. 20, 24.

Barthelme successfully mixes fantasy with "flat-footed reality." Rather than escaping, Barthelme as fabulist deals with "the vital mysteries of contemporary fact."

I29   Peden, William. *The American Short Story* (Boston: Houghton-Mifflin, 1975), pp. 12, 19, 27, 177-179, 183, 185, 188.

Commenting on collage, Barthelme indicates his method of dealing with contemporary manners and bizarre aspects of present-day life. His influence include Borges, Disney, Chester Gould, and Ingmar Bergman. Beneath it all, Barthelme is a conventional moralist commenting upon a sick society.

I30   Rother, James. "Parafiction: The Adjacent Universe of Barth, Barthelme, Pynchon, and Nabokov." *Boundary 2* 5 (Fall 1976): 21-44.

Snow White acknowledges its sources in fairy tale and film while affirming neither—hence it is a parafiction. The bulk of Barthelme's writing centers on gaps in the original story line. The fiction of life is meant to be experienced by way of words and words alone, destroying the conventional boundaries of actual life.

I31   Samuels, Charles Thomas. "Moving Through 'The Indian Uprising.'" *The Process of Fiction*, 2nd Edition. Edited by Barbara McKenzie (New York: Harcourt Brace Jovanovich, 1974), pp. 529-537.

Barthelme's story "doesn't so much dramatize an action as provide a series of notations from which it is possible to infer a dramatic shape." The key technique is cinematic montage, as in a Marx Brothers film.

I32   Schmitz, Neil. "Donald Barthelme and the Emergence of Modern Satire." *Minnesota Review* 1 (no. 4, 1972): 109-118.

An attention to our culture's fragmented use of language allows Barthelme to satirize both his subject and his own form of writing.

I33 ———. "What Irony Unravels." *Partisan Review* 40 (no. 3, 1973): 482-490.

Barthelme is the "most pure of contemporary satirists," but his ironic mode becomes in *S* the method of his confinement. His main themes are the confused life of the writer, and the confusion which blankets his world. Barthelme's result is a withdrawal into comic fantasy.

I34 Scholes, Robert. "Metafiction." *Iowa Review* 1 (Fall 1970): 100-115.

Barthelme reinvents forms which touch the vital ideas of fiction, since the older forms have atrophied. His is the "fiction of essence" which imitates other fiction (or fiction itself) as an insight into the "deep structure of being."

I35 Shadoian, Jack. "Notes on Donald Barthelme's *Snow White*." *Western Humanities Review* 24 (Winter 1970): 73-75.

SW creates the illusion of randomness. Its flawed satire disturbs its imaginative coherence.

I36 Shorris, Earl. "Donald Barthelme's Illustrated Wordy-Gurdy." *Harper's* 246 (January 1973): 92-94, 96.

Barthelme's work "makes a world that deflates the world we know, to create surpassing experience." He makes us "suddenly defenseless in the world, disarmed of the deafness, blindness, and insensitivity that insulate and preserve us." Barthelme examines society by studying its language.

I37 Stern, Daniel. "The Mysterious New Novel." *Liberations*. Edited by Ihab Hassan (Middletown, Conn.: Wesleyan University Press, 1971), pp. 31-32.

Barthelme's parody language derives from Beckett. He exhausts the "straight statements of our situations." Behind his satiric attacks is "the metaphysical mystery" of life.

I38 Stevick, Phillip. "Scheherazade Runs Out of Plots, Goes On Talking; The King, Puzzled, Listens: An Essay on the New Fiction." *TriQuarterly* no. 26 (Winter 1973), pp. 332-362.

Allegiance to earlier, inappropriate critical values makes Barthelme seem incomprehensible. His fiction is not "epiphanic" or "illuminative," as is the case with conventional Modernist writing.

I39 _____. "Lies, Fictions, and Mock Facts." *Western Humanities Review* 30 (Winter 1976): 1-12.

In "Robert Kennedy Saved From Drowning," Barthelme presents a fictional image more real than historical fact.

I40 Stott, William. "Donald Barthelme and the Death of Fiction." *Prospects* no. 1 (1975), pp. 369-386.

In an age when "nonfiction increasingly appeases our hunger for the facts of real life," Barthelme writes stories which show what happens to fiction in a nonfiction world: "what happens to private values when all facts are treated as public." His language helps achieve this result, by mixing private and public words indiscriminately.

I41 Tanner, Tony. *City of Words: American Fiction 1950-1970* (New York: Harper & Row, 1971), pp. 141, 393, 400-406.

Through his fragments Barthelme satirizes the contemporary world, which he "turns to strangeness" by fracturing our habitual arrangements and separations by which we control that life.

I42 Whalen, Tom. "Wonderful Elegance: Barthelme's 'The Party.'" *Critique* 16 (no. 3, 1975): 45-48.

"The Party" takes the form of a mosaic, made coherent by the unified setting and the reappearance of characters.

I43 Wickes, George. "From Breton to Barthelme: Westward the Course of Surrealism." *Proceedings: Pacific Northwest Conference on Foreign Languages*, 22 (1971): 208-214.

I44 Wilde, Alan. "Barthelme Unfair to Kierkegaard: Some Thoughts on Modern and Postmodern Irony." *Boundary 2* 5 (Fall 1976): 45-70.

Barthelme is less interested in fiction-making flaws in human relationships than he is in "the odd relationship between the individual mind and the humanized world of things and objects on which that mind has, collectively and precariously, left its imprint." His concerns are less epistemological than ontological.

J.

REVIEWS OF BOOKS
BY DONALD BARTHELME

J1   *Come Back, Dr. Caligari*

   Best Sellers, May 1, 1964, p. 46.
   Best Sellers, November 1, 1971, p. 363.
   Books and Bookmen, May 1966, p. 32.
   Book Week, May 31, 1964, p. 7.
   Chicago Tribune, April 5, 1964, p. 20.
   Hudson Review, Autumn 1967, pp. 473-486.
   Library Journal, June 1, 1964, p. 2363.
   Nation, June 8, 1964, pp. 583.
   New Republic, May 2, 1964, pp. 18-19.
   Newsweek, April 13, 1964, pp. 97-98.
   New York Review of Books, April 30, 1964, p. 10.
   New York Times Book Review, April 12, 1964, p. 36.
   New Yorker, June 13, 1964, p. 141.
   Saturday Night, January 1965, p. 26.
   Saturday Review, April 4, 1964, pp. 23-24.
   Saturday Review, August 28, 1965, p. 46.
   Studies in Short Fiction, Spring 1966, pp. 386-390.
   Times Literary Supplement, February 24, 1966, p. 137.
   Twentieth Century, Spring 1966, p. 64.

J2   *Snow White*

   Book List, September 1, 1967, p. 46.
   Book Week, May 21, 1967, p. 2.
   Books and Bookmen, July 1968, p. 41.

Book World, August 18, 1968, p. 17.
Books Today, June 18, 1967, p. 6.
Christian Science Monitor, June 1, 1967.
Commonweal, December 29, 1967, p. 416.
Hudson Review, Autumn 1967, pp. 473-486.
Kenyon Review, September 1967, pp. 561-568.
Kirkus Service, March 15, 1967, p. 361.
Library Journal, May 15, 1967, p. 1950.
Life, May 26, 1967, p. 6.
Manchester Guardian, April 18, 1968, p. 13.
Nation, June 19, 1967, pp. 794-795.
New Republic, June 3, 1967, pp. 27-29.
New Statesman, April 19, 1968, p. 520.
Newsweek, May 22, 1967, p. 103.
New York Review of Books, August 24, 1967, pp. 12-13.
New York Times, May 15, 1967, p. 45M.
New York Times Book Review, May 21, 1967, p. 4.
Observer, April 7, 1968, p. 24.
Observer, July 25, 1971, p. 23.
Publishers Weekly, March 13, 1967, p. 55.
Publishers Weekly, July 22, 1968, p. 64.
Saturday Review, July 1, 1967, p. 24.
Time, May 26, 1967, p. 96.
Times Literary Supplement, May 9, 1968, p. 484.
Virginia Quarterly Review, Summer 1967, p. CIV.
Wall Street Journal, July 13, 1967, p. 14.

J3 *Unspeakable Practices, Unnatural Acts*

America, June 15, 1968, p. 777.
Atlantic, July 1968, pp. 89-91.
Book List, June 15, 1968, p. 1174.
Books and Bookmen, October 1969, p. 23.
Book World, May 19, 1968, p. 3.
Book World, June 8, 1969, p. 13.
Choice, June 1969, p. 1440.
Christian Science Monitor, June 13, 1968, p. 11.
Commonweal, June 21, 1968, p. 414.
Critic, June 1968, pp. 74-76.
Hudson Review, Summer 1968, p. 364.
Kirkus Service, March 1, 1968, p. 283.
Library Journal, July 1968, p. 2687.

Listener, July 31, 1969, p. 158.
Nation, May 27, 1968, p. 703.
New Republic, June 1, 1968, pp. 34-35.
New Statesman, July 31, 1969, p. 121.
Newsweek, May 6, 1968, p. 112.
New York Review of Books, April 25, 1968, pp. 5-6.
New York Times, April 24, 1968, p. 45.
New York Times Book Review, May 12, 1968, p. 7.
Observer, August 17, 1969, p. 20.
Publishers Weekly, March 11, 1968, p. 42.
Publishers Weekly, April 7, 1969, p. 57.
Saturday Review, May 11, 1968, p. 81.
Sewanee Review, Summer 1970, pp. 539-540.
Spectator, August 2, 1969, p. 146.
Time, May 24, 1968, p. 106.
Times Literary Supplement, August 14, 1969, p. 910.

J4   *City Life*

American Librarian, January 1971, p. 124.
Antioch Review, Spring 1970, p. 129.
Atlantic, May 1970, p. 132.
Book List, June 15, 1970, p. 1380.
Book World, April 26, 1970, p. 5.
Catholic World, December 1970, pp. 159-160.
Choice, October 1970, p. 1032.
Christian Science Monitor, May 14, 1970, p. 11.
Critic, September 1970, pp. 86-87.
Esquire, December 1970, pp. 96-106.
Harper's, May 1970, p. 130.
Kirkus Service, February 15, 1970, p. 195.
Library Journal, May 1, 1970, p. 1758.
Life, May 8, 1970, p. 19.
Nation, May 25, 1970, pp. 630-631.
New Leader, June 22, 1970, pp. 20-21.
New Statesman, July 30, 1971, p. 155.
New York Times, May 1, 1970.
New York Times Book Review, April 27, 1970, p. 1.
New York Times Book Review, June 7, 1970, p. 2.
New York Times Book Review, December 6, 1970, p. 1.
Observer, August 22, 1971, p. 25.
Publishers Weekly, February 23, 1970, p. 150.

Saturday Review, May 9, 1970, p. 34.
Saturday Review, November 28, 1970, p. 30.
Studies in Short Fiction, Fall 1970, pp. 661-663.
Sewanee Review, Summer 1970, p. 531.
Time, May 25, 1970, pp. 106-108.
Time, January 4, 1971, p. 76.
Times Literary Supplement, December 3, 1971, p. 1497.
Virginia Quarterly Review, Autumn 1970, p. 129.

J5   *The Slightly Irregular Fire Engine*

Center for Children's Books, May 1972, p. 134.
Instructor, June 1973, p. 62.
Kirkus Service, August 15, 1971, p. 870.
Library Journal, October 15, 1971, p. 3456.
New York Review of Books, December 2, 1971, pp. 25-28.
New York Times, December 14, 1971, p. 43.
New York Times Book Review, November 7, 1971, pp. 1, 36-37.
New Yorker, December 4, 1971, p. 181.
Publishers Weekly, August 30, 1971, p. 274.
Time, December 27, 1971, p. 61.

J6   *Sadness*

America, October 7, 1972, p. 265.
Atlantic, December 1972, pp. 126-132.
Best Sellers, April 1975, p. 9.
Book List, January 1, 1973, p. 427.
Books and Bookmen, February 1974, p. 59.
Book World, May 30, 1971, p. 9.
Book World, December 1, 1974, p. 4.
Book World, December 22, 1974, p. 3.
Choice, March 1973, p. 87.
Cresset, April 1973, p. 11.
Harper's, January 1973, pp. 92-96.
Hudson Review, Spring 1973, p. 234.
Instructor, June 1973, p. 62.
Kirkus Service, September 1, 1972, p. 1041.
Library Journal, November 1972, p. 3613.
Listener, December 6, 1973, p. 793.

National Observer, November 4, 1972, p. 21.
National Review, December 22, 1972, pp. 1413-1414.
New Republic, November 11, 1972, pp. 28-29.
Newsweek, November 6, 1972, pp. 128-129.
New York Review of Books, December 14, 1972, p. 12.
New York Times, October 27, 1972, p. 39.
New York Times Book Review, November 5, 1972, pp. 27-31.
Observer, December 9, 1973, p. 36.
Publishers Weekly, September 4, 1972, p. 41.
Saturday Review, November 25, 1972, p. 66.
Spectator, December 8, 1973, p. 746.
Time, November 27, 1972, p. 95.
Times Literary Supplement, December 7, 1973, p. 1495.
World, November 7, 1972, p. 65.

J7 *Guilty Pleasures*

America, March 29, 1975, p. 44.
Atlantic, December 1974, p. 128.
Best Sellers, December 15, 1974, p. 405.
Book List, January 5, 1975, p. 480.
Book World, November 3, 1974, p. 3.
Book World, December 15, 1974, p. 1.
Book World, March 7, 1976, p. 8.
Choice, February 1975, p. 1774.
Christian Science Monitor, January 2, 1975, p. 10.
Kirkus Service, September 15, 1974, p. 1027.
Kirkus Service, October 1, 1974, p. 1071.
National Observer, November 30, 1974, p. 24.
National Review, March 28, 1975, p. 357.
New Republic, December 14, 1974, p. 22.
Newsweek, November 25, 1974, p. 117.
New York Times, November 2, 1974, p. 27.
New York Times Book Review, November 3, 1974, p. 7.
Publishers Weekly, September 16, 1974, p. 58.
Time, November 11, 1974, pp. 111-112.
Virginia Quarterly Review, Spring 1975, p. 54.

J8 *The Dead Father*

Antioch Review, Spring 1976, p. 368.
Atlantic, December 1975, p. 112.

Best Sellers, January 1976, p. 308.
Book List, June 1, 1975, p. 612.
Chicago Daily News, November 8, 1975, p. 6.
Choice, March 1976, p. 64.
Chronicle of Higher Education, December 22, 1975, p. 20.
Commonweal, June 4, 1976, p. 379.
Kirkus Service, September 15, 1975, p. 1081.
Library Journal, November 15, 1975, p. 2170.
National Observer, December 27, 1975, p. 17.
New Republic, November 29, 1975, p. 35.
Newsweek, November 3, 1975, p. 89.
New York Times, November 3, 1975, p. 33.
New York Times Book Review, December 7, 1975, p. 62.
New York Times Book Review, December 28, 1975, p. 1.
New Yorker, November 24, 1975, p. 194.
New York Review of Books, December 11, 1975, pp. 1, 54.
Publishers Weekly, September 29, 1975, p. 44.
Village Voice, November 3, 1975, p. 51.
Yale Review, March 1976, p. 404.

J9   *Amateurs*

Booklist, December 1, 1976, p. 525.
Charleston Evening Post, November 28, 1976, p. 17.
Detroit Free Press, October 31, 1976, p. 10.
Houston Chronicle, January 9, 1977, p. 8.
Kirkus Service, October 15, 1976, p. 1187.
Library Journal, December 15, 1976, p. 1278.
Los Angeles Times, November 28, 1976, p. 5.
New York Times, November 23, 1976, p. 31.
New York Times Book Review, December 19, 1976, p. 17.
New Yorker, December 13, 1976, p. 162.
Newsweek, November 29, 1976, p. 103.
News & Observer (Raleigh, NC), December 12, 1976, p. 12.
Philadelphia Sunday Bulletin, December 26, 1976, p. 4.
Playboy, January 1977, p. 40.
Saturday Review/World, December 11, 1976, p. 69.
Villager, November 11, 1976, p. 37.
Washington Post Book World, November 28, 1976, p. 3.

K.

PUBLICLY DISAVOWED FORGERIES OF STORIES ALLEGEDLY WRITTEN BY "DONALD BARTHELME"

K1 "Divorce." *Carolina Quarterly* 25 (Fall 1973): 52-59.

K2 "Cannon!" *Voyages* 5 (no. 1-4, 1973): 62-67.

K3 "Cannon!" *Georgia Review* 27 (Winter 1973): 566-572. Text differs slightly.

K4 "Cannon!" *Ann Arbor Review* no. 17 (1973), pp. 65-71. Text differs slightly from both previous versions.

K5 "Sentence Passed on the Show of a Nations's Brain Damage, etc. Or, The Autobiography of a Crime." *December* 15 (no. 1-2, 1973): 83-94.

INDEX

"Adventure," B62
"The Affront," AB1, B27
"After Joyce," C12
"The Agreement," B121
"Alexandria and Henrietta," B75
"Alice," B39
Alpaca, C4
Alvarez, Jose Manuel, AA8, AC9, AD6
Amateurs, AI, B55, B64, B95, B96, B97, B98, B99, B101, B102, B104, B105, B107, B114, B115, B119, B120, B121, B122, B125, B127, B128, B140, J9
American Place Theatre, D1
"And Now Let's Hear It For the Ed Sullivan Show," B46
"And Then," B107
"The Angry Young Man," B94
Ann Arbor Review, K4
Ansel, Ruth AH1
Architectural Graphics, C5
Art and Literature, B12, B24
Atlantic, B83, B99, B125, B134
"At the End of the Mechancial Age," B99
"At the Tolstoy Museum," B47
Audience, B82

"The Balloon," B31, I16a
Barklund, Gunnar, AD7

"The Bed," B113
"Belief," B143
Bierhorst, Jane, AC1, AE 1
"The Big Broadcast of 1938," B3
Bonacina, Giancarlo, AB8
"Bone Bubbles," B50
Bosse-Sporleder, Maria, AB6
Bradbury, Christopher, AB4
"Brain Damage," B53
"Bunny Image, Loss Of: The Case of Bitsy S.," B118

"Can We Talk," B24
"Cannon!", K2, K3, K4
"The Captured Woman," B140
Carano, Ranieri, AC6
Carolina Quarterly, K1
"The Case of the Vanishing Product," C7
"The Catechist," B74
Chapman, Stanley, AC4, AD4
City Life, AD, B37, B40, B42, B44, B45, B47, B48, B49, B50, B52, B53, B54, B58, F2, I8, J4
"City Life," B44
"City Life II," B45
"A City of Churches," B80
Come Back, Dr. Caligari, AA, B1, B2, B3, B4, B6, B7, B8, B9, B10, B11, B12, B15, B16, B17, F2, J1

The Comedians, C13
"Comment," B57, B78, B108, B110, B116, B123, B124, B129, B130, B131, B132, B139, B141, B142
Contact, B1, B4
Contemporary Arts Museum, C5, C6, C8, C9, C11
Cordier & Eckstrom, C15
"Cornell," B136
"Critique de la Vie Quotidienne," B70
"Culture etc.," C3

"The Darling Duckling at School," B1
"The Dassaud Prize," B133
"Daumier," B79
Davis, Keith, AI3
The Dead Father, AH, B75, B126, F2, J8
"The Death of Edward Lear," B64
December, K5
"Departures," B73
"The Discovery," B102
"Divorce," K1
"The Dolt," B35
"Down the Line With the Annual," B13
"The Dragon," B78
"A Dream," B103

"The Educational Experience," B98
"Edward and Pia," B26
"Edwards, Amelia," B84
"Elaine de Kooning Paints a Picture," C10
"The Elegance Is Under Control," C14
The Emerging Figure, C6
"Engineer-Private Paul Klee Misplaces an Aircraft Between Milbertshofen and Cambrai, March 1916," B66
Esquire, B46
"Eugenie Grandet," B41
"The Expedition," B82
"The Explanation," B37

"The Falling Dog," B40
"A Few Moments of Sleeping and Waking," B34
Fiction, B86, B94, B128, E2
"A Film," B57, B61
First Person, B2
Fleckhaus, Willy, AB6, AC5
"The Flight of Pigeons From the Palace," B60
"Florence Green is 81," B6
"Flying to America" B57, B76
"For I'm the Boy," B15
Ford, Harry, AB3
Forsstrom, Ingmar, AC7
Forum (University of Houston), B143, C1, C2, C6, E3

"Game," B23
"Games Are the Enemy of Beauty, Truth and Sleep, Amanda Said," B32
Genesis West, B8
"The Genius," B65
Georgia Review, K3
Galbraith, John Kenneth, C14
Glaser, Milton, AA1, AA3
"The Glass Mountain," B58, I16a
Gorey, Edward, AA2
Gorlier, Claudio, AA6
"The Great Debate," B138
"The Great Hug," B127
Greene, Graham, C13
Groot, Patricia de, AD1
Guilty Pleasures, AG, B5, B13, B25, B32, B41, B46, B56, B76, B78, B82, B88, B92, B93, B94, B100, B103, B106, B108, B109, B111, B112, B116, B117, B118, E1, J7

Harper's, B71, B91, B98, B107, C7
Harper's Bazaar, B6, B62
Halverson, Janet, AC1
"Heliotrope," B116
"An Hesitation on the Banks of the Delaware," B103
"The Hiding Man," B2
Hills, Rust, C16
Holiday, C13

Hollman-Steffa, Liisa, AB10
Hoog, Else, AB9
Hunt, H. L., C4

"I Bought a Little City," B122
"The Inauguration," B91
"The Indian Uprising," B22, I2

Jaskari, Juhani, AC8
"The Joker's Greatest Triumph," B16

"Kierkegaard Unfair to Schlegel," B42
Klinkowitz, Jerome, H1, H2

"L'Lapse," B5
"Letters to the Editore," B112
Lish, Gordon, F1
Location, B15, C12, E2, E3
Louchivaara, Kyllikki, AB10

"A Made Up Story," B92
Mademoiselle, B32
"A Man," B90
"Manfred," B137
"A Manual for Sons," B126
"Man's Face," B14
"Margins," B11
"Marie, Marie, Hold On Tight," B9
McCaffery, Larry, H3
McNeil, Lily [pseudonym of Donald Barthelme], B100, B103, B106, F2
"Me and Miss Mandible," B1
"Mr. Foolfarm's Journal," B117
"Mr. Hunt's Woolly Utopia," C4
"Monumental Folly," B134
"The Mothball Fleet," B72
"Mother," B21
"Mouth," B50
Muschg, Hanna und Adolf, AC5

"A Nation of Wheels," B56
"Natural History," B71
New American Review, B36, B75
"The New Member," B120
New Sounds in American Fiction, F1

"Newsletter," B59
New World Writing, B3
New York Times, B88, B106
New York Times Book Review, C14
New York Times Magazine, B93, B135, B137
New Yorker, B5, B7, B9-11, B13-14, B18-20, B22-23, B25-26, B28-29, B31, B33-35, B37-38, B41-45, B47-49, B51-57, B59-61, B63-70, B72-74, B76-81, B84, B87, B89-90, B92, B95-97, B100-105, B108-112, B114, B116, B119-126, B129-133, B138-142, E1, E3, I18
"A Note on Elia Kazan," C1
"Nothing: A Preliminary Account," B109

Oellers, Marianne, AD5
"On Angels," B48
"One Hundred Ten West 61st Street," B104
"Our Work and Why We Do It," B96
"Over the Sea of Hesitation," B89

Pacifica Tape Library, F2
"The Palace," B108
"Pages from the Annual Report," C2
"Paraguay," B49, C16
Paris Review, B30, B39, B50
"The Party," B77, I42
Perez, Angela, AA8, AC9, AD6
"Perpetua," B69
Petersen, Arne Herlov, AC10
"The Phantom of the Opera's Friend," B52
"Philadelphia," B43
"The Photographs," B111
"The Piano Player," B7, F1
"A Picture History of the War," B18
Playboy, B115
"The Police Band," B19
"The Policemen's Ball," B38

"Porcupines at the University," B55
"The President," B20

Ratzkin, Lawrence, AB1
"Rebecca," B125
"The Reference," B115
"Reiner, David," C2
"Report," B33
Reporter, C4
"The Rise of Capitalism," B63
"Robert Kennedy Saved From Drowning," B36, I21, I39
"Robert Morris," C17
"The Royal Treatment," B106

Sadness, AF, B57, B59, B60, B61, B63, B65, B66, B68, B69, B70, B73, B74, B77, B79, B80, B81, B83, B85, I33, J6
"The Sandman," B83
"The School," B119
"See the Moon?", B29
"Sentence," B54
"Sentence Passed on the Show of a Nation's Brain Damage, etc. Or The Autobiography of a Crime," K5
"The Sergeant," B128
"Several Garlic Tales," AB1, B30
she, C15
"The Short Story Contest," B135
"The Show," B60
"A Shower of Gold," B10
The Slightly Irregular Fire Engine, AE, F2, J5
"Snap Snap," B25
Snow White, AB, B30, D1, F2, I6, I8, I10, I13, I19, I21, I24, I25, I30, I35, J2
"Some of Us Had Been Threatening Our Friend Colby," B97
"The Story Thus Far," B67
"Subpoena," B68
"Swallowing," B88
"Symposium on Fiction," C18

"The Teachings of Don B.: A Yankee Way of Knowledge," B93
"The Temptation of St. Anthony," B81
Texas Observer, C3
"That Cosmopolitan Girl," B100
"Then," B21
"This Newspaper Here," B28
"Three," B86
Tibor, Bartos, AA9
"The Tired Terror of Graham Greene," C13
"To London and Rome," B8
"Traumerei," B85
The Triumph, C14
"Two Hours to Curtain," B57, B76

University of Houston Forum (see *Forum*)
Unspeakable Practices, Unnatural Acts, AC, B18, B19, B20, B22, B23, B24, B26, B28, B29, B30, B32, B34, B35, B36, B38, B39, I8, J3
"Up, Aloft in the Air," B17

"The Viennese Opera Ball," B4
"Views of My Father Weeping," B51, I21
Village Voice, B117
Viva, B113
Voyages, K2

Ways and Means, C8
"What To Do Next," B95
"Will You Tell Me?", B12
Wollschlager, Hans, AA5, AA7
"The Wound," B105
"Wrack," B87
Writer's Choice, C16

"You Are as Brave as Vincent Van Gogh," B114
"You Are Cordially Invited," B101
"The Young Visitirs," [sic], B92

Zins, Céline, AB7, AC11